Smiles@n_,.- .....

A smorgasbord of my amusing,
entertaining and interesting
e-mails

Jamie Doggart

ISBN – 13: 978 – 1499523669
ISBN – 10: 1499523661

I gratefully acknowledge the kindness of all those friends who have included me in their mailing lists and helped brighten up even the dullest of days.

What Causes Arthritis?

A drunk man who smelled like beer sat down on a subway next to a priest. The man's tie was stained, his face was plastered with red lipstick and a half empty bottle of gin was sticking out out his torn coat pocket. He opened his newspaper and began reading.

After a few minutes the man turned to the priest and asked, "Say Father, what causes arthritis?"
The priest, wanting to teach this man a little lesson replied, "My son, it's caused by loose living, being with cheap, wicked women, too much alcohol, contempt for your fellow man, sleeping around with prostitutes and lack of a bath."

The drunk muttered in response, "Well, I'll be damned," then returned to his paper.

The priest, thinking about what he had said, nudged the man and apologised. "I'm very sorry. I didn't mean to come on so strong. How long have you had arthritis?"

The drunk answered, "I don't have it, Father. I was just reading here that the Pope does."

☺   @   ☺

Pregnant?

A woman went to the doctor's office, where she was seen by a young, new doctor. After about 4 minutes in the examination room, the doctor told her she was pregnant. She burst out, screaming as she ran down the hall.

An older doctor stopped her and asked what the problem was, and she told him her story. After listening, he had her sit down and relax in another room.

The doctor marched down the hallway to the back where the first doctor was and demanded, "What's the matter with you? Mrs. Smith is 59 years old, she has four grown children and seven grandchildren, and you told her she was pregnant?"

The new doctor continued to write on his clipboard and without looking up said, "And does she still have the hiccups?"

☺ @ ☺

Mt. Rushmore from the Canadian Side

Always wondered what was on the other side . . .

☺ @ ☺

My neighbour knocked on my door at 2:30 am this morning, can you believe that 2:30 am? Luckily for him I was still up playing my Bagpipes.

☺ @ ☺

Redneck Vacation

Billy Bob and Luther were talking one afternoon when Billy Bob tells Luther,

"Ya know, I reckon I'm 'bout ready for a vacation. Only this year I'm gonna do it a little different. The last few years, I took your advice about where to go.

Three years ago you said to go to Hawaii . I went to Hawaii and Earlene got pregnant.

Then two years ago, you told me to go to the Bahamas , and Earlene got pregnant again.

Last year you suggested Tahiti and darned if Earlene didn't get pregnant again."

Luther asks Billy Bob, "So, what you gonna do this year that's different?"

Billy Bob says, "This year I'm taking Earlene with me."

Questions to haunt you . . .

Can you cry under water?

How important does a person have to be before they are considered assassinated instead of just murdered?

Why do you have to 'put your two cents in'... but it's only a 'penny for your thoughts'? Where's that extra penny going to?

Once you're in heaven, do you get stuck wearing the clothes you were buried in for eternity?

Why does a round pizza come in a square box?

What disease did cured ham actually have?

How is it that we put man on the moon before we figured out it would be a good idea to put wheels on luggage?

Why is it that people say they 'slept like a baby' when babies wake up like every two hours?

If a deaf person has to go to court, is it still called a hearing?

Why are you IN a film, but you're ON TV?

Why do people pay to go up tall buildings and then put money in binoculars to look at things on the ground?

Why do doctors leave the room while you change?
They're going to see you naked anyway...

Why is 'bra' singular and 'pants' plural?

Why do toasters always have a setting that burns the toast to a horrible crisp, which no decent human being would eat?

If Jimmy cracks corn and no one cares, why is there a stupid song about him?

Why does Goofy stand erect while Pluto remains on all fours? They're both dogs!

If corn oil is made from corn, and vegetable oil is made from vegetables, what is baby oil made from?

If electricity comes from electrons, does morality come from morons?

Did you ever notice that when you blow in a dog's face, he gets angry with you, but when you take him for a car ride, he sticks his head out the window?

Why, Why, Why . . .

. . . do we press harder on a remote control when we know the batteries are getting dead?

Why do banks charge a fee on 'insufficient funds' when they know there is not enough money?

Why does someone believe you when you say there are four billion stars, but check when you say the paint is wet?

Why do they use sterilized needles for death by lethal injection?

Why doesn't Tarzan have a beard?

Why does Superman stop bullets with his chest, but ducks when you throw a revolver at him?

Why do Kamikaze pilots wear helmets?

Have you noticed that all the people in favour of birth control are already born?

If people evolved from apes, why are there still apes?

Why is it that no matter what colour bubble bath you use the bubbles are always white?

Is there ever a day that mattresses are not on sale?

Why do people constantly return to the refrigerator with hopes that something new to eat will have materialized?

Why do people keep running over a string a dozen times with their vacuum cleaner, then reach down, pick it up, examine it, then put it down to give the vacuum one more chance?

Why is it that no plastic bag will open from the end on your first try?

How do those dead bugs get into those enclosed light fixtures?

Why is it that whenever you attempt to catch something that's falling off the table you always manage to knock something else over?

In winter why do we try to keep the house as warm as it was in summer when we complained about the heat?

How come you never hear father-in-law jokes?

Mother and her young inquisitive son were flying Singapore Airlines from Singapore to Sydney. The son (who had been looking out the window) turned to his mother and asked, "If dogs have baby dogs and cats have baby cats, why don't planes have baby planes?"

The mother (who couldn't think of an answer) told her son to ask the pretty flight attendant. So the boy dutifully asked the flight attendant, "If dogs have baby dogs and cats have baby cats, why don't planes have baby planes?"

The flight attendant responded, "Did your mother tell you to ask me that?" The little boy admitted that she did.

"Well, then, tell your mother that there are no baby planes because Singapore Airlines always pulls out on time.

Now, let your mother explain that to you."

Only a Farm Kid . . .

When you're from the country, your perception is a little bit different.

A farmer drove to a neighbour's farmhouse and knocked at the door.
A boy, about 9, opened the door
"Is your dad or mum home?" said the farmer.
"No, they went to town."
"How about your brother, Howard? Is he here?"
"No, he went with Mum and Dad."
The farmer stood there for a few minutes, shifting from one foot to the other, and mumbling to himself.
"I know where all the tools are, if you want to borrow one, or I can give Dad a message."
"Well," said the farmer uncomfortably, "I really wanted to talk to your Dad. It's about your brother Howard getting my daughter Suzy pregnant".

The boy thought for a moment... "You would have to talk to Dad about that. I know he charges $500 for the bull and $50 for the pig, but I don't know how much he charges for Howard."

☺ @ ☺

Chinese Logic

Henry Kissinger once asked Chou En-Lai to theorize on what might have happened if Nikita Khrushchev had been assassinated instead of John F. Kennedy.

After a moment's thought, Chou En-Lai answered: "I don't believe Mr. Onassis would have married Mrs. Khrushchev."

☺ @ ☺

All you Need to Know about Government Bureaucracy:--

Pythagorean Theorem:	24 words.
Lord's Prayer:	66 words.
Archimedes' Principle:	67 words.
10 Commandments:	179 words.
Gettysburg Address:	286 words.
US Declaration of Independence :	1,300 words.
US Constitution with all 27 Amendments:	7,818 words.
EU regulations on the sale of cabbage:	26,911 words.

SORT OF PUTS THINGS INTO PROPER PERSPECTIVE, DOESN'T IT?

☺ @ ☺

Awaiting . . .

With breathless anticipation the crowd awaits the unveiling of the new statue to Tony Blair.

☺ @ ☺

During his physical examination, a doctor asked a man about his physical activity level.
He described a typical day this way:
"Well, yesterday afternoon, I took a five hour walk about 7km through some pretty rough terrain. I waded along the edge of a lake. I pushed my way through brambles. I got sand in my shoes and my eyes. I avoided standing on a snake. I climbed several rocky hills. I took a few 'leaks' behind some big trees. The mental stress of it all left me shattered. At the end of it all I drank eight beers"
Inspired by the story, the doctor said,
"You must be one hell of an outdoors man!"
"No," he replied, "I'm just a rubbish golfer".

Morality of Dishonesty

A few years ago robbers entered a bank in a small town.

One of them shouted: "Don't move! The money belongs to the bank. Your lives belong to you."

Immediately all the people in the bank laid on the floor quietly and without panic.

This is an example of how the correct wording of a sentence can make everyone change their view of the world.

One woman lay on the floor in a provocative manner.

The robber approached her saying, " Ma'am, this is a robbery not a rape. Please behave accordingly."

This is an example of how to behave professionally, and focus on the goal.

While running from the bank the youngest robber (who had a college degree) said to the oldest robber (who had barely finished elementary school): "Hey, maybe we should count how much we stole."?

The older man replied: "Don't be stupid. It's a lot of money so let's wait for the news on TV to find out how much money was taken from the bank."

This is an example of how life experience is more important than a degree.

After the robbery, the manager of the bank said to his accountant:

"Let's call the police and tell them how much has been stolen."

"Wait", said the Accountant, "before we do that, let's add the $800,000 we took for ourselves a few months ago and just say that it was stolen as part of today's robbery."

This is an example of taking advantage of an opportunity.

The following day it was reported in the news that the bank was robbed of $ 3 million.

The robbers counted the money, but they found only $1 million so they started to grumble.

"We risked our lives for $1 million, while the bank's management robbed two million dollars without blinking? Maybe its better to learn how to work the system, instead of being a simple robber."

This is an example of how knowledge can be more useful than power.

Moral :Give a person a gun, and he can rob a bank . Give a person a bank, and he can rob everyone.

☺   @   ☺

I sat in my armchair and shouted to my wife, "When I die I'm going to leave everything to you, my love!"

She shouts back: "You already do, you lazy b******d"

How to Give your Cat a Pill

1. Pick cat up and cradle it in the crook of your left arm as if holding a baby. Position right forefinger and thumb on either side of cat's mouth and gently apply pressure to cheeks while holding pill in right hand. As cat opens mouth, pop pill into mouth. Allow cat to close mouth and swallow.

2. Retrieve pill from floor and cat from behind sofa. Cradle cat in left arm and repeat process.

3. Retrieve cat from bedroom, and throw soggy pill away.

4. Take new pill from foil wrap, cradle cat in left arm holding rear paws tightly with left hand. Force jaws open and push pill to back of mouth with right forefinger. Hold mouth shut for a count of ten.

5. Retrieve pill from goldfish bowl and cat from top of wardrobe. Call spouse from yard.

6. Kneel on floor with cat wedged firmly between knees, hold front and rear paws. Ignore low growls emitted by cat. Get spouse to hold head firmly with one hand while forcing wooden ruler into mouth. Drop pill down ruler and rub cat's throat vigorously.

7. Retrieve cat from curtain rail, get another pill from foil wrap. Make note to buy new ruler and repair curtains. Carefully sweep shattered figurines and vases from hearth and set to one side for gluing later.

8. Wrap cat in large towel and get spouse to lie on cat with head just visible from below armpit. Put pill in end of drinking straw, force mouth open with pencil and blow down drinking straw.

9. Check label to make sure pill not harmful to humans, drink one beer to take taste away. Apply Band-Aid to spouse's forearm and remove blood from carpet with cold water and soap.

10. Retrieve cat from neighbour's shed. Get another pill. Open another beer. Place cat in cupboard and close door onto neck to leave head showing. Force mouth open with dessert spoon. Flick pill down throat with rubber band.

11. Fetch screwdriver from garage and put cupboard door back on hinges. Drink beer. Fetch bottle of Scotch. Pour shot, drink. Apply cold compress to cheek and check records for date of last tetanus shot. Apply whisky compress to cheek to disinfect. Toss back another shot. Throw tee-shirt away and fetch new one from bedroom.

12. Call fire department to retrieve the cat from tree across the road. Apologize to neighbour who crashed into fence while swerving to avoid cat. Take last pill from foil-wrap.

13. Tie the darn thing's front paws to rear paws with twine and bind tightly to leg of dining room table, find heavy duty pruning gloves from shed. Push pill into mouth followed by large piece of steak. Be rough about it. Hold head vertically and pour two pints of water down throat to wash pill down.

14. Consume remainder of Scotch. Get spouse to drive you to emergency room, sit quietly while doctor stitches fingers and forearm and removes pill remnants from right eye. Call furniture shop on way home to order new table.

15. Arrange for Humane Society to collect cat and call local pet shop to see if they have any hamsters.

How to Give a Dog a Pill

1. Wrap it in bacon

Seeing is believing

Stare at the above picture carefully. Is he looking straight at you or right to left?

Fishing

After 35 years of marriage, a husband and wife went in for counselling. When asked what the problem was, the wife went into a passionate, painful tirade listing every problem they had ever had in the years they had been married.

She went on and on and on: neglect, lack of intimacy, emptiness, loneliness, feeling unloved and unlovable, an entire laundry list of unmet needs she had endured.

Finally, after allowing this for a sufficient length of time, the therapist got up, walked around the desk and after asking the wife to stand, embraced and kissed her passionately as her husband watched with a raised eyebrow.

The woman shut up and quietly sat down as though in a daze. The therapist turned to the husband and said, 'this is what your wife needs at least 3 times a week Can you do this?'

"Well, I can drop her off here on Mondays and Wednesdays, but on Fridays, I go fishing," replied the husband.

☺ @ ☺

How the word `Boob' was invented

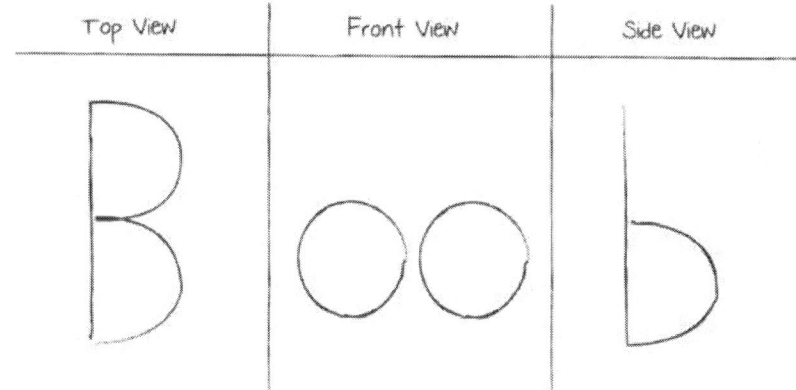

Makes sense to me.

☺ @ ☺

Senior Sense

We went to breakfast at a restaurant where the 'seniors' special' was two eggs, bacon, hash browns and toast with tea or coffee for £2.99.

'Sounds good,' my wife said. 'But I don't want the eggs.'

'Then, I'll have to charge you £3.49 because you're ordering a la carte,' the waitress warned her.

'You mean I'd have to pay for not taking the eggs?' my wife asked incredulously.

'YES!' stated the waitress.

'I'll take the special then,' my wife said..

'How do you want your eggs?' the waitress asked.

'Raw and in the shell,' my wife replied. She took the two eggs home and baked a cake.

DON'T MESS WITH SENIORS!!!
WE'VE been around the block more than once!

☺ @ ☺

Neologisms

Once again, The Washington Post has published the winning submissions to its yearly neologism contest, in which readers are asked to supply alternative meanings for common words.

The winners are:

1. Coffee (n.), the person upon whom one coughs.

2. Flabbergasted (adj.), appalled over how much weight you have gained.

3. Abdicate (v.), to give up all hope of ever having a flat stomach.

4. Esplanade (v.), to attempt an explanation while drunk.

5. Willy-nilly (adj.), impotent.

6. Negligent (adj.), a condition in which you absent-mindedly answer the door in your nightgown.

7. Lymph (v.), to walk with a lisp.

8. Gargoyle (n), olive-flavoured mouthwash.

9. Flatulence (n.) emergency vehicle that picks you up after you are run over by a steamroller.

10. Balderdash (n.), a rapidly receding hairline.

11. Testicle (n.), a humorous question on an exam.

12. Rectitude (n.), the formal, dignified bearing adopted by proctologists.

13. Pokemon (n), Rastafarian proctologist.

14. Oyster (n.), person who sprinkles his conversation with Yiddishisms.

15. Frisbeetarianism (n.), (back by popular demand): The belief that, when you die, your soul flies up onto the roof and gets stuck there.

16. Circumvent (n.), opening in the front of boxer shorts worn by Jewish men.

The Washington Post's Style Invitational also asked readers to take any word from the dictionary, alter it by adding, subtracting, or changing one letter, and supply a new definition.

Here are this year's winners:

1. Bozone (n.): The substance surrounding stupid people that stops bright ideas from penetrating. The bozone layer, unfortunately, shows little sign of breaking down in the near future.

2. Foreploy (v): Any misrepresentation about yourself for the purpose of getting laid.

3. Cashtration (n.): The act of buying a house, which renders the subject financially impotent for an indefinite period.

4. Giraffiti (n): Vandalism spray-painted very, very high.

5. Sarchasm (n): The gulf between the author of sarcastic wit and the person who doesn't get it.

6. Inoculatte (v): To take coffee intravenously when you are running late.

7. Hipatitis (n): Terminal coolness.

8. Osteopornosis (n): A degenerate disease. (that one got extra credit)

9. Karmageddon (n): Its like, when everybody is sending off all these really bad vibes, right? And then, like, the Earth explodes and it's like, a serious bummer.

10. Decafalon (n.): The gruelling event of getting through the day consuming only things that are good for you.

11. Glibido (v): All talk and no action.

12. Dopeler effect (n): The tendency of stupid ideas to seem smarter when they come at you rapidly.

13. Arachnoleptic fit (n.): The frantic dance performed just after you've accidentally walked through a spider web.

14. Beelzebug (n.): Satan in the form of a mosquito that gets into your bedroom at three in the morning and cannot be cast out.

15. Caterpallor (n.): The colour you turn after finding half a grub in the fruit you're eating.

And the pick of the literature:

16. Ignoranus (n): A person who's both stupid and an asshole.

☺   @   ☺

A Boy, a Man and a Donkey

An old man, a boy & a donkey were going to town. The boy rode on the donkey & the old man walked. As they went along they passed some people who remarked it was a shame the old man was walking and the boy was riding. The man and boy thought maybe the critics were right, so they changed positions. Then, later, they passed some people who remarked, 'What a shame, he makes that little boy walk.' So they then decided they'd both walk!

Soon they passed some more people who thought they were stupid to walk when they had a decent donkey to ride. So, they both rode the donkey.

Now they passed some people who shamed them by saying how awful to put such a load on a poor donkey. The boy and man figured they were probably right, so they decide to carry the donkey. As they crossed the bridge, they lost their grip on the animal and he fell into the river and drowned.

The moral of the story?

If you try to please everyone, You might as well...
Kiss your ass goodbye!

Kulula Airline

WHAT A PITY KULULA DOESN'T FLY INTERNATIONALLY - WE SHOULD SUPPORT THEM IF ONLY FOR THEIR HUMOUR - SO TYPICALLY SOUTH AFRICAN.

Kulula is an Airline with head office situated in Johannesburg .

Kulula airline attendants make an effort to make the in-flight "safety lecture" and announcements a bit more entertaining. Here are some real examples that have been heard or reported:

On a Kulula flight, (there is no assigned seating, you just sit where you want) passengers were apparently having a hard time choosing, when a flight attendant announced, "People, people we're not picking out furniture here, find a seat and get in it!"

---ooo---

On another flight with a very "senior" flight attendant crew, the pilot said, "Ladies and gentlemen, we've reached cruising altitude and will be turning down the cabin lights. This is for your comfort and to enhance the appearance of your flight attendants."

----ooo---

On landing, the stewardess said, "Please be sure to take all of your belongings.. If you're going to leave anything, please make sure it's something we'd like to have."

----ooo---

"There may be 50 ways to leave your lover, but there are only 4 ways out of this airplane."

---ooo---

"Thank you for flying Kulula. We hope you enjoyed giving us the business as much as we enjoyed taking you for a ride."

---ooo---

As the plane landed and was coming to a stop at Durban Airport , a lone voice came over the loudspeaker: "Whoa, big fella. WHOA!"

---ooo---

After a particularly rough landing during thunderstorms in the Karoo , a flight attendant on a flight announced, "Please take care when opening the overhead compartments because, after a landing like that, sure as hell everything has shifted."

---ooo---

From a Kulula employee: " Welcome aboard Kulula 271 to Port Elizabeth . To operate your seat belt, insert the metal tab into the buckle, and pull tight. It works just like every other seat belt; and, if you don't know how to operate one, you probably shouldn't be out in public unsupervised."

---ooo---

"In the event of a sudden loss of cabin pressure, masks will descend from the ceiling. Stop screaming, grab the mask, and pull it over your face. If you have a small child travelling with you, secure your mask before assisting with theirs. If you are travelling with more than one small child, pick your favourite."

---ooo---

"Weather at our destination is 50 degrees with some broken clouds, but we'll try to have them fixed before we arrive. Thank you, and remember, nobody loves you, or your money, more than Kulula Airlines."

"Your seats cushions can be used for flotation; and in the event of an emergency water landing, please paddle to shore and take them with our compliments."

---ooo---

"As you exit the plane, make sure to gather all of your belongings. Anything left behind will be distributed evenly among the flight attendants. Please do not leave children or spouses.."

---ooo---

And from the pilot during his welcome message: "Kulula Airlines is pleased to announce that we have some of the best flight attendants in the industry. Unfortunately, none of them are on this flight!"

---ooo---

Heard on Kulula 255 just after a very hard landing in Cape Town : The flight attendant came on the intercom and said, "That was quite a bump and I know what y'all are thinking. I'm here to tell you it wasn't the airline's fault, it wasn't the pilot's fault, it wasn't the flight attendant's fault, it was the asphalt."

---ooo---

Overheard on a Kulula flight into Cape Town , on a particularly windy and bumpy day, during the final approach, the Captain really had to fight it. After an extremely hard landing, the Flight Attendant said, "Ladies and Gentlemen, welcome to The Mother City. Please remain in your seats with your seat belts fastened while the Captain taxis what's left of our airplane to the gate!"

---ooo---

Another flight attendant's comment on a less than perfect landing: "We ask you to please remain seated as Captain Kangaroo bounces us to the terminal."

---ooo---

An airline pilot wrote that on this particular flight had hammered his ship into the runway really hard. The airline had a policy which required the first officer to stand at the door while the passengers exited, smile, and give them a "Thanks for flying our airline." He said that, in light of his bad landing, he had a hard time looking the passengers in the eye, thinking that someone would have a smart comment. Finally everyone had gotten off except for a little old lady walking with a cane. She said, "Sir, do you mind if I ask you a question?" "Why, no Ma'am," said the pilot. "What is it?" The little old lady said, "Did we land, or were we shot down?"

---ooo---

After a real crusher of a landing in Johannesburg , the attendant came on with, "Ladies and Gentlemen, please remain in your seats until Captain Crash and the Crew have brought the aircraft to a screeching halt against the gate. And, once the tyre smoke has cleared and the warning bells are silenced, we will open the door and you can pick your way through the wreckage to the terminal.."

---ooo---

Part of a flight attendant's arrival announcement: "We'd like to thank you folks for flying with us today.. And, the next time you get the insane urge to go blasting through the skies in a pressurized metal tube, we hope you'll think of Kulula Airways."

---ooo---

Heard on a Kulula flight. "Ladies and gentlemen, if you wish to smoke, the smoking section on this airplane is on the wing.. If you can light 'em, you can smoke 'em."

---ooo---

A plane was taking off from Durban Airport . After it reached a comfortable cruising altitude, the captain made an announcement over the intercom, "Ladies and gentlemen, this is your captain speaking. Welcome to Flight Number 293, non-stop from Durban to Cape Town , The weather ahead is good and, therefore, we should have a smooth and uneventful flight.. Now sit back and relax... OH, MY GOODNESS!" Silence followed, and after a few minutes, the captain came back on the intercom and said, "Ladies and Gentlemen, I am so sorry if I scared you earlier. While I was talking to you, the flight attendant accidentally spilled a cup of hot coffee in my lap. You should see the front of my pants!" A passenger then yelled, "That's nothing. You should see the back of mine."

☺ @ ☺

Tom's Scrotum

The pastor asked if anyone in the congregation would like to express praise for answered prayers. Suzie Smith stood and walked to the podium.

She said, "I have a praise. Two months ago, my husband, Tom, had a terrible bicycle wreck and his scrotum was completely crushed. The pain was excruciating and the doctors didn't know if they could help him." You could hear a muffled gasp from the men in the congregation as they imagine the pain that poor Tom must have experienced. "Tom was unable to hold me or the children," she went on, "and every move caused him terrible pain."

We prayed as the doctors performed a delicate operation, and it turned out they were able to piece together the crushed remnants of Tom's scrotum, and wrap wire around it to hold it in place." Again, the men in the congregation cringed and squirmed uncomfortably as they imagined the horrible surgery performed on Tom. "Now," she announced in a quivering voice, "thank the Lord, Tom is out of the hospital and the doctors say that with time, his scrotum should recover completely."

All the men sighed with unified relief. The pastor rose and tentatively asked if anyone else had something to say. A man stood up and walked slowly to the podium.

He said, "I'm Tom Smith." The entire congregation held its breath.

"I just want to tell my wife the word is sternum."

HELL EXPLAINED

By A Chemistry Student

The following is an actual question given on a University of Arizona chemistry midterm, and an actual answer turned in by a student.

The answer by one student was so 'profound' that the professor shared it with colleagues, via the Internet, which is, of course, why we now have the pleasure of enjoying it as well.

Bonus Question:

Is Hell exothermic (gives off heat) or endothermic (absorbs heat)?

Most of the students wrote proofs of their beliefs using Boyle's Law (gas cools when it expands and heats when it is compressed) or some variant.

One student, however, wrote the following:

First, we need to know how the mass of Hell is changing in time. So we need to know the rate at which souls are moving into Hell and the rate at which they are leaving, which is unlikely.

I think that we can safely assume that once a soul gets to Hell, it will not leave. Therefore, no souls are leaving. As for how many souls are entering Hell, let's look at the different religions that exist in the world today.

Most of these religions state that if you are not a member of their religion, you will go to Hell. Since there is more than one of these religions and since people do not belong to more than one religion, we can project that all souls go to Hell. With birth and death rates as they are, we can expect the number of souls in Hell to increase exponentially.

Now, we look at the rate of change of the volume in Hell because Boyle's Law states that in order for the temperature and pressure in Hell to stay the same, the volume of Hell has to expand proportionately as souls are added.

This gives two possibilities:

1. If Hell is expanding at a slower rate than the rate at which souls enter Hell, then the temperature and pressure in Hell will increase until all Hell breaks loose.

2. If Hell is expanding at a rate faster than the increase of souls in Hell, then the temperature and pressure will drop until Hell freezes over.

So which is it?

If we accept the postulate given to me by Teresa during my Freshman year that, 'It will be a cold day in Hell before I sleep with you,' and take into account the fact that I slept with her last night, then number two must be true, and thus I am sure that Hell is exothermic and has already frozen over. The corollary of this theory is that since Hell has frozen over, it follows that it is not accepting any more souls and is therefore, extinct..... ...leaving only Heaven, thereby proving the existence of a divine being which explains why, last night, Teresa kept shouting 'Oh my God.'

THIS STUDENT RECEIVED AN A+

☺   @   ☺

When I Say I'm Broke - I'm Broke!

A little old lady answered a knock on the door one day, to be confronted by a well-dressed young man carrying a vacuum cleaner.
'Good morning,' said the young man. 'If I could take a couple minutes of your time, I would like to demonstrate the very latest in high-powered vacuum cleaners...
"Go away!" said the old lady. "I'm broke and haven't got any money!" and she proceeded to close the door.
Quick as a flash, the young man wedged his foot in the door and pushed it wide open... "Don't be too hasty!" he said. "Not until you have at least seen my demonstration."
And with that, he emptied a bucket of horse manure onto her hallway carpet.
Now if this vacuum cleaner does not remove all traces of this horse manure from your carpet, Madam, I will personally eat the remainder."
The old lady stepped back and said, "well let me get you a fork, 'cause they cut off my electricity this morning."

☺   @   ☺

Secretary Requires Help from Design Team with Reference to her Missing Cat:

From: Shannon Walkley
Date: Monday 21 June 2010 9.15am
To: David Thorne
Subject: Poster

Hi

I opened the screen door yesterday and my cat got out and has been missing since then so I was wondering if you are not to busy you could make a poster for me. It has to be A4 and I will photocopy it and put it around my suburb this afternoon.

This is the only photo of her I have she answers to the name Missy and is black and white and about 8 months old. missing on Harper street and my phone number.

Thanks Shan.

From: David Thorne
Date: Monday 21 June 2010 9.26am
To: Shannon Walkley
Subject: Re: Poster

Dear Shannon,

That is shocking news. Luckily I was sitting down when I read your email and not half way up a ladder or tree. How are you holding up? I am surprised you managed to attend work at all what with thinking about Missy out there cold, frightened and alone... possibly lying on the side of the road, her back legs squashed by a vehicle, calling out "Shannon, where are you?"

Although I have two clients expecting completed work this afternoon, I will, of course, drop everything and do whatever it takes to facilitate the speedy return of Missy.

Regards, David.

From: Shannon Walkley
Date: Monday 21 June 2010 9.37am
To: David Thorne
Subject: Re: Re: Poster

yeah ok thanks. I know you don't like cats but I am really worried about mine. I have to leave at 1pm today.

From: David Thorne
Date: Monday 21 June 2010 10.17am
To: Shannon Walkley
Subject: Re: Re: Re: Poster

Dear Shannon, I never said I don't like cats. Once, having been invited to a party, I went clothes shopping beforehand and bought a pair of expensive G-Star boots. They were two sizes too small but I wanted them so badly I figured I could just wear them without socks and cut my toenails very short. As the party was only a few blocks from my place, I decided to walk. After the first block, I lost all feeling in my feet. Arriving at the party, I stumbled into a guy named Steven, spilling Malibu & coke onto his white Wham 'Choose Life' t-shirt, and he punched me.

An hour or so after the incident, Steven sat down in a chair already occupied by a cat. The surprised cat clawed and snarled causing Steven to leap out of the chair, slip on a rug and strike his forehead onto the corner of a speaker; resulting in a two inch open gash.

In its shock, the cat also defecated, leaving Steven with a foul stain down the back of his beige cargo pants. I liked that cat.

Attached poster as requested.

Regards, David.

From: Shannon Walkley
Date: Monday 21 June 2010 10.24am
To: David Thorne
Subject: Re: Re: Re: Re: Poster

yeah thats not what I was looking for at all. it looks like a movie and how come the photo of Missy is so small?

From: David Thorne
Date: Monday 21 June 2010 10.28am
To: Shannon Walkley
Subject: Re: Re: Re: Re: Re: Poster

Dear Shannon,

It's a design thing. The cat is lost in the negative space.

Regards, David.

From: Shannon Walkley
Date: Monday 21 June 2010 10.33am
To: David Thorne
Subject: Re: Re: Re: Re: Re: Re: Poster

Thats just stupid. Can you do it properly please? I am extremely emotional over this and was up all night in tears. you seem to think it is funny. Can you make the photo bigger please and fix the text and do it in colour please. Thanks.

From: David Thorne
Date: Monday 21 June 2010 10.46am
To: Shannon Walkley
Subject: Re: Re: Re: Re: Re: Re: Re: Poster

Dear Shannon,

Having worked with designers for a few years now, I would have assumed you understood, despite our vague suggestions otherwise, we do not welcome constructive criticism. I don't come downstairs and tell you how to send text messages, log onto Facebook and look out of the window. I am willing to overlook this faux pas due to you no doubt being preoccupied with thoughts of Missy attempting to make her way home across busy intersections or being trapped in a drain as it slowly fills with water. I spent three days down a well once but that was just for fun.

I have amended and attached the poster as per your instructions.

Regards, David.

From: Shannon Walkley
Date: Monday 21 June 2010 10.59am
To: David Thorne
Subject: Re: Re: Re: Re: Re: Re: Re: Re: Poster

This is worse than the other one. can you make it so it shows the whole photo of Missy and delete the stupid text that says missing missy off it? I just want it to say Lost.

From: David Thorne
Date: Monday 21 June 2010 11.14am
To: Shannon Walkley
Subject: Re: Re: Re: Re: Re: Re: Re: Re: Poster

From: Shannon Walkley
Date: Monday 21 June 2010 11.21am
To: David Thorne
Subject: Re: Re: Re: Re: Re: Re: Re: Re: Re: Poster

yeah can you do the poster or not? I just want a photo and the word lost and the telephone number and when and where she was lost and her name. Not like a movie poster or anything stupid. I have to leave early today. If it was your cat I would help you. Thanks.

From: David Thorne
Date: Monday 21 June 2010 11.32am
To: Shannon Walkley
Subject: Awww

Dear Shannon,

I don't have a cat. I once agreed to look after a friend's cat for a week but after he dropped it off at my apartment and explained the concept of kitty litter, I kept the cat in a closed cardboard box in the shed and forgot about it. If I wanted to feed something and clean faeces, I wouldn't have put my mother in that home after her stroke. A week later, when my friend came to collect his cat, I pretended that I was not home and mailed the box to him. Apparently I failed to put enough stamps on the package and he had to collect it from the post office and pay eighteen dollars. He still goes on about that sometimes, people need to learn to let go.

I have attached the amended version of your poster as per your detailed instructions.

Regards, David.

LOST

MISSY THE CAT
MISSING FROM HARPER STREET ON THE 20TH OF JUNE
CONTACT 0433 359 705

From: Shannon Walkley
Date: Monday 21 June 2010 11.47am
To: David Thorne
Subject: Re: Awww

That's not my cat. where did you get that picture from? That cat' is entirely different. I gave you a photo of my cat.

From: David Thorne
Date: Monday 21 June 2010 11.58am
To: Shannon Walkley
Subject: Re: Re: Awww

I know, but that one is cute. As Missy has quite possibly met any one of several violent ends, it is possible you might get a better cat out of this.

If anybody calls and says "I haven't seen your orange cat but I did find a black and white one with its hind legs run over by a car, do you want it?" you can politely decline and save yourself a costly veterinarian bill.

I knew someone who had a basset hound that had its hind legs removed after an accident and it had to walk around with one of those little buggies with wheels.

If it had been my dog I would have asked for all its legs to be removed and replaced with wheels and had a remote control installed.

I could charge neighbourhood kids for rides and enter it in races. If I did the same with a horse I could drive it to work. I would call it Steven.

Regards, David.

From: Shannon Walkley
Date: Monday 21 June 2010 12.07pm
To: David Thorne
Subject: Re: Re: Re: Awww

Please just use the photo I gave you.

From: David Thorne
Date: Monday 21 June 2010 12.22pm
To: Shannon Walkley
Subject: Re: Re: Re: Re: Awww

LOST

MISSY THE CAT
REWARD OFFERED
$2000
MISSING FROM HARPER STREET
ON THE 20TH OF JUNE

CONTACT 0433 359 705

From: Shannon Walkley
Date: Monday 21 June 2010 12.34pm
To: David Thorne
Subject: Re: Re: Re: Re: Re: Awww

I didn't say there was a reward. I don't have $2000 dollars. What did you even put that there for? Apart from that it is perfect can you please remove the reward bit. Thanks Shan.

From: David Thorne
Date: Monday 21 June 2010 12.42pm
To: Shannon Walkley
Subject: Re: Re: Re: Re: Re: Re: Awww

LOST

MISSY THE CAT
NO REWARD

MISSING FROM HARPER STREET ON THE 20TH OF JUNE

CONTACT 0433 359 705

From: Shannon Walkley
Date: Monday 21 June 2010 12.51pm
To: David Thorne
Subject: Re: Re: Re: Re: Re: Re: Re: Awww

Can you just please take the reward bit off altogether? I have to leave in ten minutes and I still have to make photocopies of it.

From: David Thorne
Date: Monday 21 June 2010 12.56pm
To: Shannon Walkley
Subject: Re: Re: Re: Re: Re: Re: Re: Re: Awww

LOST

MISSY THE CAT

MISSING FROM HARPER STREET ON THE 20TH OF JUNE

CONTACT 0433 359 705

From: Shannon Walkley
Date: Monday 21 June 2010 1.03pm
To: David Thorne
Subject: Re: Re: Re: Re: Re: Re: Re: Re: Re: Awww

Fine. That will have to do.

☺ @ ☺

A Small Glimmer of Hope

'Viagra' is now available in powder form for your tea.
It doesn't enhance your sexual performance . . .
but it does stop your biscuit going soft..

☺ @ ☺

A Moral/Ethical Question

You are driving down the road in your Corvette on a wild, stormy night, when you pass by a bus stop and you see three people waiting for the bus:

1. An old lady who looks as if she is about to die.

2. An old friend who once saved your life.

3. The perfect partner you have been dreaming about.

Which one would you choose to offer a ride to, knowing that there could only be one passenger in your car? Think before you continue reading.

This is a moral/ethical dilemma that was once actually used as part of a job application. You could pick up the old lady, because she is going to die, and thus you should save her first. Or you could take the old friend because he once saved your life, and this would be the perfect chance to pay him back. However, you may never be able to find your perfect mate again.

YOU WON'T BELIEVE THIS......................

The candidate who was hired (out of 200 applicants) had no trouble coming up with his answer. He simply answered: 'I would give the car keys to my old friend and let him take the lady to the hospital. I would stay behind and wait for the bus with the partner of my dreams.'

Sometimes, we gain more if we are able to give up our stubborn thought limitations.

Never forget to 'Think Outside of the Box.'

However . . .

. . . the correct answer is to run the old lady over and put her out of her misery, have sex with the perfect partner on the bonnet of the car, then drive off with the old friend for a few beers.

☺ @ ☺

MATRIMONY?

You have two choices in life:
You can stay single and be miserable,
or get married and wish you were dead.
_____

At a cocktail party, one woman said to another,
"Aren't you wearing your wedding ring on the wrong finger?"
"Yes, I am. I married the wrong man."
_____

A lady inserted an ad in the classifieds:
"Husband Wanted".
Next day she received a hundred letters.
They all said the same thing:
"You can have mine."
_____

When a woman steals your husband,
there is no better revenge than to let her keep him.
_____

A woman is incomplete until she is married. Then she is finished
_____

A little boy asked his father,
"Daddy, how much does it cost to get married?"
Father replied, "I don't know son, I'm still paying."
_____

A young son asked,
"Is it true Dad, that in some parts of Africa
a man doesn't know his wife until he marries her?"
Dad replied, "That happens in every country, son."
_____

Then there was a woman who said,
"I never knew what real happiness was until I got married, and by then, it was too late."

Marriage is the triumph of imagination over intelligence.

If you want your spouse to listen and
pay strict attention to every word you say -- talk in your sleep.

Just think, if it weren't for marriage, men would go through life thinking they had no faults at all.

First guy says, "My wife's an angel!"
Second guy remarks, "You're lucky, mine's still alive."

AND NOW FOR MY FAVOURITE!!!

Husband and wife are waiting at the bus stop with their nine children. A blind man joins them after a few minutes. When the bus arrives, they find it overloaded and only the wife and the nine kids are able to fit onto the bus.
So the husband and the blind man decide to walk. After a while, the husband gets irritated by the ticking of the stick of the blind man as he taps it on the sidewalk, and says to him, "Why don't you put a piece of rubber at the end of your stick? That ticking sound is driving me crazy."
The blind man replies, "If you had put a rubber at the end of YOUR stick, we'd be riding the bus, so shut up.

☺   @   ☺

A Conundrum

If New Age Travellers are so keen on travelling,
why do they always make such a fuss when they get moved on?

☺   @   ☺

A (supposedly) True Story

For those who have served on a jury...this one is something to think about. Just when you think you have heard everything!!

Do you like to read a good murder mystery? Not even Law and Order would attempt to capture this mess. This is an unbelievable twist of fate!!!!

At the 1994 annual awards dinner given for Forensic Science, (AAFS) President, Dr. Don Harper Mills astounded his audience with the legal complications of a bizarre death. Here is the story:

On March 23,1994, the medical examiner viewed the body of Ronald Opus and concluded that he died from a shotgun wound to the head. Mr. Opus had jumped from the top of a ten-story building intending to commit suicide.

He left a note to the effect indicating his despondency. As he fell past the ninth floor, his life was interrupted by a shotgun blast passing through a window, which killed him instantly.

Neither the shooter nor the deceased was aware that a safety net had been installed just below the eighth floor level to protect some building workers and that Ronald Opus would not have been able to complete his suicide the way he had planned.

The room on the ninth floor, where the shotgun blast emanated, was occupied by an elderly man and his wife. They were arguing vigorously and he was threatening her with a shotgun! The man was so upset that when he pulled the trigger, he completely missed his wife, and the pellets went through the window, striking Mr. Opus.

When one intends to kill subject 'A' but kills subject 'B' in the attempt, one is guilty of the murder of subject 'B.'

When confronted with the murder charge, the old man and his wife were both adamant, and both said that they thought the shotgun was not loaded. The old man said it was a long-standing habit to threaten his wife with the unloaded shotgun. He had no intention to murder her. Therefore the killing of Mr. Opus appeared to be an accident; that is, assuming the gun had been accidentally loaded.

The continuing investigation turned up a witness who saw the old couple's son loading the shotgun about six weeks prior to the fatal accident. It transpired that the old lady had cut off her son's financial support and the son, knowing the propensity of his father to use the shotgun threateningly, loaded the gun with the expectation that his father would shoot his mother.

Since the loader of the gun was aware of this, he was guilty of the murder even though he didn't actually pull the trigger. The case now becomes one of murder on the part of the son for the death of Ronald Opus.

Now comes the exquisite twist.... Further investigation revealed that the son was, in fact, Ronald Opus.

He had become increasingly despondent over the failure of his attempt to engineer his mother's murder. This led him to jump off the ten-story building on March 23rd, only to be killed by a shotgun blast passing through the ninth story window.

The son, Ronald Opus, had actually murdered himself. So the medical examiner closed the case as a suicide.

☺ @ ☺

I was driving this morning when I saw an RAC van parked up, the driver was sobbing uncontrollably and looked very miserable. I thought to myself 'that guy's heading for a breakdown'.

☺ @ ☺

Careful With Your Wallet

This Scam was sent to me by a friend. I thought it wise to pass on to all men out there.

A ' heads up ' for those men who may be regular customers at B&Q, Morrison 's or even Focus. This one caught me totally by surprise. Over the last month I became a victim of a clever scam while out shopping. Simply going out to get supplies has turned out to be quite traumatic.

Don't be naive enough to think it couldn't happen to you or your friends..

Here's how the scam works:

Two nice-looking, college-aged girls will come over to your car as you are packing your purchases into your vehicle. They both start wiping your windscreen with a sponge and leather, with their breasts almost falling out of their skimpy T-shirts. (It ' s impossible not to look). When you thank them and offer them a tip, they say ' No thanks", but instead ask for a ride to McDonalds.

You agree and they climb into the car. On the way, they start undressing.

Then one of them starts crawling all over you, exposing herself and using intimate hand caresses - while the other one steals your wallet.

I had my wallet stolen on September 4th, 9th, 10th, twice on the 15th, 17th, 20th, 24th, & 29th.

Also on October 1st & 4th, twice on the 8th, 16th, 23rd, 26th & 27th, and very likely again this upcoming weekend.

PS:

Wilko has wallets on sale for £2.99 each. I found even cheaper ones for 99p at the Pound Shop and cleaned them out in three of their shops.

Also, as you never get to actually eat at McDonald's. I've already lost 11 pounds just running back and forth from Focus, B&Q and Wilko..

So please, send this on to all the older men that you know and warn them to be on the lookout for this scam. (The best times are just before lunch and around 4:30 in the afternoon.)

☺ @ ☺

Second Opinion

The doctor said, 'Joe, the good news is I can cure your headaches. The bad news is that it will require castration.

You have a very rare condition, which causes your testicles to press on your spine and the pressure creates one hell of a headache. The only way to relieve the pressure is to remove the testicles.'

Joe was shocked and depressed. He wondered if he had anything to live for. He had no choice but to go under the knife. When he left the hospital, he was without a headache for the first time in 20 years, but he felt like he was missing an important part of himself. As he walked down the street, he realized that he felt like a different person. He could make a new beginning and live a new life.

He saw a men's clothing store and thought, 'That's what I need... A new suit...'

He entered the shop and told the salesman, 'I'd like a new suit..'

The elderly tailor eye d him briefly and said, 'Let's see... Size 44 long.'

Joe laughed, 'That's right, how did you know?'

'Been in the business 60 years!' the tailor said.

Joe tried on the suit it fit perfectly.

As Joe admired himself in the mirror, the salesman asked, 'How about a new shirt?'

Joe thought for a moment and then said, 'Sure.'

The salesman eyed Joe and said, 'Let's see, 34 sleeves and 16-1/2 neck.'

Joe was surprised, 'That's right, how did you know?'

'Been in the business 60 years.'

Joe tried on the shirt and it fit perfectly.

Joe walked comfortably around the shop and the salesman asked, 'How about some new underwear?'

Joe thought for a moment and said, 'Sure.'

The salesman said, 'Let's see... Size 36.

Joe laughed, 'Ah ha! I got you! I've worn a size 34 since I was 18 years old.'

The salesman shook his head, 'You can't wear a size 34. A size 34 would press your testicles up against the base of your spine and give you one hell of a headache.'

☺ @ ☺

A Rare Occurrence

There was a knock on the door this morning, I opened it and there was a young bloke standing there who said:

"I'm a Jehovah's Witness".

I said "Come in and sit down, what do you want to talk about"?

He said, " Blowed if I know, I've never got this far before".

☺ @ ☺

Grandparents' Answering Machine

Good morning. At present we are not at home, but please leave your message after the beep.

If you are one of our children, dial 1 and then select the option from 1 to 5 in order of "arrival" so we know who it is.

If you need us to stay with the children, press 2
If you want to borrow the car, press 3
If you want us to wash your clothes and ironing, press 4
If you want the grandchildren to sleep here tonight, press 5
If you want us to pick up the kids at school, press 6
If you want us to prepare a meal for Sunday or to have it delivered to your home, press 7
If you want to come to eat here, press 8
If you need money, press 9

If you are inviting us to dinner, or taking us to the theatre, start talking - we are listening!"

☺ @ ☺

National Stereotyping Alert

On a beautiful deserted island in the middle of nowhere, the following group of people are shipwrecked :-

2 Italian men and 1 Italian woman
2 French men and 1 French woman
2 German men and 1 German woman
2 Greek men and 1 Greek woman
2 Bulgarian men and 1 Bulgarian woman
2 Japanese men and 1 Japanese woman
2 Chinese men and 1 Chinese woman
2 Australian men and 1 Australian woman
2 Irish men and 1 Irish woman
2 English men and 1 English woman

One month later on the same island in the middle of nowhere, the following things have occurred:

One Italian man killed the other Italian man for the Italian woman.

The two French men and the French woman are living happily together in a ménage-à-trois.

The two German men have a strict weekly schedule of alternating visits with the German woman.

The two Greek men are sleeping with each other and the Greek woman is cleaning and cooking for them.

The two Bulgarian men took one long look at the ocean, another long look at the Bulgarian woman, and started swimming.

The two Japanese men have faxed Tokyo and are awaiting instructions.

The two Chinese men have set up a pharmacy, a liquor store, a restaurant and a laundry, and have got the woman pregnant in order to supply employees for their stores.

The two Australian men are contemplating suicide because the Australian woman keeps complaining about her body; the true nature of feminism; how she can do everything they can do; the necessity of fulfilment; the equal division of household chores; how sand and palm trees make her look fat; how her last boyfriend respected her opinion and treated her nicer than they do; how her relationship with her mother is improving, and how at least the taxes are low and it isn't raining.

The two Irish men have divided the island into North and South and have set up a distillery. They do not remember if sex is in the picture because it gets sort of foggy after the first few litres of coconut whisky. But they're satisfied because at least the English aren't having any fun.

The two English men are waiting for someone to introduce them to the English woman.

☺ @ ☺

How Is Norma?

A sweet grandmother telephoned St. Joseph's Hospital. She timidly asked, "Is it possible to speak to someone who can tell me how a patient is doing?"

The operator said, "I'll be glad to help, dear. What's the name and room number of the patient?"

The grandmother in her weak, tremulous voice said, "Norma Findlay, Room 302."

The operator replied, "Let me put you on hold while I check with the nurse's station for that room."

After a few minutes, the operator returned to the phone and said, "I have good news. Her nurse just told me that Norma is doing well. Her blood pressure is fine; her blood work just came back normal and her Physician, Dr. Cohen, has scheduled her to be discharged tomorrow."

The grandmother said, "Thank you. That's wonderful. I was so worried. God bless you for the good News."

The operator replied, "You're more than welcome. Is Norma your daughter?"

The grandmother said,"No, I'm Norma Findlay in Room 302. No one tells me anything."

☺   @   ☺

Texas Beer Joint Sues Church In Mt.Vernon, Texas.

Drummond's Bar began construction on expansion of their building to increase their business.

In response, the local Baptist Church started a campaign to block the bar from expanding with petitions and prayers. Work progressed right up until the week before the grand reopening when lightning struck the bar and it burned to the ground!

After the bar burning to the ground by a lightning strike, the church folks were rather smug in their outlook, bragging about "the power of prayer ", until the bar owner sued the church on the grounds that the church . . ."was ultimately responsible for the demise of his building, either through direct or indirect actions or means."

In its reply to the court, the church vehemently denied all responsibility or any connection to the building's demise.

The judge read through the plaintiff's complaint and the defendant's reply, and at the opening hearing he commented "I don't know how I'm going to decide this, but it appears from the paperwork that we have a bar owner who believes in the power of prayer, and an entire church congregation that now does not."

☺ @ ☺

Letter from Irish Mother to her Son

Dear Son,

Just a few lines to let you know I'm still alive. I'm writing this letter slowly because I know you can't read fast. We are all doing very well.

You won't recognize the house when you get home - we have moved. Your dad read in the newspaper that most accidents happen within 20 miles from your home, so we moved. I won't be able to send you the address because the last Irish family that lived here took the house numbers when they moved so that they wouldn't have to change their address.

This place is really nice. It even has a washing machine. I'm not sure it works so well though: last week I put a load in and pulled the chain and haven't seen them since..

Your father's got a really good job now. He's got 500 men under him. He's cutting the grass at the cemetery.

Your sister Mary had a baby this morning but I haven't found out if it's a boy or a girl, so I don't know whether you are an auntie or an uncle.

Your brother Tom is still in the army. He's only been there a short while and they've already made him a court martial!

Your Uncle Patrick drowned last week in a vat of whisky in the Dublin Brewery. Some of his workmates tried to save him but he fought them off bravely. They cremated him and it took three days to put out the fire.

I'm sorry to say that your cousin Seamus was arrested while riding his bicycle last week. They are charging him with dope peddling. I went to the doctor on Thursday and your father went with me. The doctor put a small tube in my mouth and told me not to talk for ten minutes. Your father offered to buy it from him.

The weather isn't bad here. It only rained twice this week, first for three days and then for four days. Monday was so windy one of the chickens laid the same egg four times. We had a letter from the undertaker. He said if the last payment on your grandmother's plot wasn't paid in seven days, up she comes.

About that coat you wanted me to send you, your Uncle Stanley said it would be too heavy to send in the mail with the buttons on, so we cut them off and put them in the pockets.

John locked his keys in the car yesterday. We were really worried because it took him two hours to get me and your father out.

Three of your friends went off a bridge in a pick-up truck. Ralph was driving. He rolled down the window and swam to safety. Your other two friends were in the back. They drowned because they couldn't get the tailgate down.

There isn't much more news at this time.. Nothing much has happened..

Your loving Mum.

P.S. I was going to send you some money but I had already sealed the envelope.

A Touching Golf Story

Jim stood over his tee shot on the 450 yard 18th hole for what seemed an eternity. He waggled, looked up, looked down, waggled again, but didn't start his back swing. Finally his exasperated partner asked, 'What the hell is taking so long?'

'My wife is watching me from the clubhouse balcony,' Jim explained. 'I want to make a perfect shot.'

His partner said, 'You don't have a chance in hell of hitting her from here.'

☺ @ ☺

Adoption

A couple from a circus go to an adoption agency, but social workers are doubtful about their accommodation. So they produce photos of their 15 metre long caravan, the back half of which is a beautifully equipped nursery.

The social workers then are doubtful about the education that would be provided.

"We've employed an Oxford don who'll teach the child all the subjects, along with Mandarin and ICT skills".

Then there are doubts expressed about the child's healthy upbringing.

"Our full time nanny is an expert in paediatric welfare and diet", they reply. So the social workers are finally satisfied, and ask what age of child they were looking for.

"It doesn't really matter", they say, "so long as he fits in the cannon".

Understanding Engineers

Two engineering students were biking across a university campus when one said, "Where did you get such a great bike?"

The second engineer replied, "Well, I was walking along yesterday, minding my own business, when a beautiful woman rode up on this bike, threw it to the ground, took off all her clothes and said, "Take what you want."

The first engineer nodded approvingly and said, "Good choice: The clothes probably wouldn't have fitted you anyway."

❖

To the optimist, the glass is half-full. To the pessimist, the glass is half-empty. To the engineer, the glass is twice as big as it needs to be.

❖

What is the difference between mechanical engineers and civil engineers? Mechanical engineers build weapons. Civil engineers build targets.

❖

The graduate with a science degree asks, "Why does it work?"
The graduate with an engineering degree asks, "How does it work?"
The graduate with an accounting degree asks, "How much will it cost?"
The graduate with an arts degree asks, "Do you want fries with that?"

❖

Three engineering students were gathered together discussing who must have designed the human body.

One said, "It was a mechanical engineer. Just look at all the joints."

Another said, "No, it was an electrical engineer. The nervous system has many thousands of electrical connections."

The last one said, "No, actually it had to have been a civil engineer. Who else would run a toxic waste pipeline through a recreational area?"

❖

Normal people believe that if it ain't broke, don't fix it. Engineers believe that if it ain't broke, it doesn't have enough features yet.

❖

Two engineers were standing at the base of a flagpole, looking at its top.

A woman walked by and asked what they were doing.

"We're supposed to find the height of this flagpole," said Sven, "but we don't have a ladder."

The woman took a wrench from her purse, loosened a couple of bolts, and laid the pole down on the ground. Then she took a tape measure from her pocketbook, took a measurement, announced, "Twenty one feet, six inches," and walked away.

One engineer shook his head and laughed, "A lot of good that does us. We ask for the height and she gives us the length!"

☺ @ ☺

Bank Job

On Friday, A hooded robber burst into a bank and, at gunpoint, forced the tellers to load their cash into a plain brown bag.

As the robber approached the door, one brave customer grabbed the hood and pulled it off, revealing the robber's face. Without a moment's hesitation, the robber shot the customer.

He then looked around the bank and noticed one of the tellers looking straight at him. The robber instantly shot & killed her also. Everyone in the bank, by now horrified, stared down at the floor in silence.

The robber yelled, "Well, did anyone else see my face?"

There was a long moment of dead silence in which everyone was terrified to speak.

Then, one old Australian named Bernie cautiously raised his hand and said, "My wife got a pretty good look at you !!!!."

☺ @ ☺

Cute Story

A father put his three-year old daughter to bed, told her a story, and listened to her prayers which ended by saying,

"God bless Mummy, God bless Daddy, God bless Grandma and good-bye Grandpa."

The father asked, 'Why did you say good-bye Grandpa?'

The little girl said, "I don't know, Daddy. It just seemed like the thing to do."

The next day Grandpa died. The father thought it was a strange coincidence.

A few months later the father put the girl to bed and listened to her prayers which went like this, "God bless Mummy, God Bless Daddy and good-bye Grandma."

The next day the grandmother died.

"Holy Mackerel," thought the father, "this kid is in contact with the other side."

Several weeks later when the girl was going to bed the dad heard her say, "God bless Mummy and good-bye Daddy."

He practically went into shock. He couldn't sleep all night and got up at the crack of dawn to go to his office.

He was nervous as a cat all day, had lunch, and watched the clock.

He figured if he could get by until midnight he would be okay.

He felt safe in the office, so instead of going home at the end of the day he stayed there, drinking coffee, looking at his watch, and jumping at every sound. Finally, midnight arrived; he breathed a sigh of relief and went home.

When he got home his wife said, "I've never seen you work so late. What's the matter?"

He said, "I don't want to talk about it. I've just spent the worst day of my life."

She said, "You think you had a bad day, you'll never believe what happened to me... This morning my golf pro dropped dead in the middle of my lesson!"...

Holiday Complaints

From Thomas Cook Holidays listing some of their UK clientele's genuine complaints.

1. "I think it should be explained in the brochure that the local store in Indian villages does not sell proper biscuits like custard creams or ginger nuts."

2. "It's lazy of the local shopkeepers to close in the afternoons. I often needed to buy things during 'siesta' time -- this should be banned."

3. "On my holiday to Goa in India, I was disgusted to find that almost every restaurant served curry. I don't like spicy food at all."

4. "We booked an excursion to a water park but no-one told us we had to bring our swimming costumes and towels."

7. "The beach was too sandy."

8. "We found the sand was not like the sand in the brochure. Your brochure shows the sand as yellow but it was white."

10. "Topless sunbathing on the beach should be banned. The holiday was ruined as my husband spent all day looking at other women."

12. "No-one told us there would be fish in the sea. The children were startled."

13. "There was no egg-slicer in the apartment."

14. "We went on holiday to Spain and had a problem with the taxi drivers as they were all Spanish."

15. "The roads were uneven.."

16. "It took us nine hours to fly home from Jamaica to England. It took the Americans only three hours to get home."

17. "I compared the size of our one-bedroom apartment to our friends' three-bedroom apartment and ours was significantly smaller."

18. "The brochure stated: 'No hairdressers at the accommodation'. We're trainee hairdressers -- will we be OK staying there?"

19. "There are too many Spanish people. The receptionist speaks Spanish. The food is Spanish. Too many foreigners now live abroad."

20. "We had to queue outside with no air-conditioning."

21. "It is your duty as a tour operator to advise us of noisy or unruly guests before we travel."

22. "I was bitten by a mosquito. No-one said they could bite."

23. "My fiancé and I booked a twin-bedded room but we were placed in a double-bedded room. We now hold you responsible for the fact that I find myself pregnant. This would not have happened if you had put us in the room that we booked."

☺ @ ☺

We spend the first twelve months of our children's lives teaching them to walk and talk and the next twelve telling them to sit down and shut up.
-- *Phyllis Diller*

Cornish Tax Problems

A copy of a letter from a Cornishman to HMRC asking a simple question!

Dear HM Revenue & Customs,

My name is Denzil Pennburthy and I live in Camborne, Cornwall. I would like to present before you the following story:

Many years ago, I married a widow out of love, who had a 18-year-old daughter. After the wedding, my father came to visit a number of times, and suddenly he fell in love with my step-daughter.

My father eventually married her without my authorization. As a result, my step-daughter legally became my step-mother and my father my son-in-law.

My father's wife (also my step-daughter) and my step-mother, gave birth to a son who is my grandchild because I am the husband of my step-daughter's wife.

This boy is also my brother, as the son of my father. All at once, my wife became a grandmother, because she is the mother of my father's wife. Therefore, it appears that I am also my wife's grandchild.

A short time after these events, my wife gave birth to a son, who became my father's brother-in-law, the step-son of my father's wife, and my uncle.

My son is also my step-mother's brother, and through my step-mother, my wife has become a grandmother and I have become my own grandfather.

In light of the above mentioned, I would like to know the following:

Does my son, who is also my uncle, my father's son-in-law, and my step-mother's brother fulfil the requirements for receiving childcare benefits?

Sincerely yours,

Denzil Pennburthy.

☺ @ ☺

An Arab walks into a bar...

A rich Arab walks into a bar and is about to order a drink when he sees a guy close by wearing a Jewish cap, a prayer shawl/tzitzis and traditional locks of hair. He doesn't have to be an Einstein to know that this guy is Jewish.

So, he shouts over to the bartender so loudly that everyone can hear, "Drinks for everyone in here, bartender, but not for the Jew over there."

Soon after the drinks have been handed out, the Jew gives him a big smile, waves at him, then says, "Thank you!" in an equally loud voice.

This infuriates the Arab.

He once again loudly orders drinks for everyone except the Jew.

As before, this does not seem to bother the Jewish guy. He continues to smile, and again yells, "Thank you!"

The Arab asks the bartender, "What the hell is the matter with that Jew? I've ordered two rounds of drinks for everyone in the bar but him, and all the silly bugger does is smile and thank me. Is he nuts?"

"Nope," replies the bartender. "He owns the place."

English Humour at its Best

For those who do not listen to the 'Today' programme on Radio 4, this is English humour at its best.

Right at the end of a programme recently, there was a discussion about the obscene cost of entry into Premiership football games, the cheapest price of £60 and £100 per game is not uncommon.

An older chap being interviewed said he could recall many years ago arriving at the turnstiles (it was probably West Ham United): "That will be ten quid, mate".

"What?!" the old chap said "I could get a woman for that!"

The guy on the turnstile retorted, "Not for 45 minutes each way with a brass band and a meat pie in the interval, you wouldn't!"

Even John Humphries had a giggle.

☺ @ ☺

Practical Tips (No Guarantees!)

1. Rub your ears to boost energy: Instead of reaching for another cup of coffee, give your ears a gentle self-massage. According to Chinese medicine, stimulating the pressure points in the ears increases blood circulation to all parts of the body, giving you an instant energy boost.

2. Cure hiccups with peanut butter: Chewing and swallowing the sticky spread will interrupt your breathing pattern and force your diaphragm to relax.

3. Use honey to soothe a sore throat: A natural antibacterial and antifungal agent, honey can help coat and soothe sore throats and alleviate minor coughs.

4. Blow-dry waterlogged ears: Put a hair dryer on the gentlest setting and hold it a few inches away from your ear. The increased airflow will help to evaporate the water in your ear.

5. Make warts disappear with garlic: Garlic - which has been shown to have antiviral, antibacterial and antifungal properties - is thought to be an effective home remedy for warts. Apply a freshly cut garlic clove to the wart, place a bandage over it, and leave the bandage on overnight. Repeat every night until the wart disappears.

6. Blow on your thumb to calm jangled nerves: The thumb has its own pulse, and blowing on the thumb will cool down the thumb and thus calm the heart rate, as cold air can slow down your pulse. This trick might also help simply because the act of blowing forces you to deepen your breathing, which calms the heart.

7. Sniff peppermint to quell a craving: Chew mint gum, sip peppermint tea or take a whiff of peppermint oil. Studies suggest that the scent of peppermint stimulates the brain to release appetite-suppressing hormones and promotes a feeling of fullness.

8. Curl your toes to fall asleep faster: The next time you find yourself tossing and turning, try a progressive muscle relaxation technique. Begin by slowly curling and uncurling your toes. Then, work your way up the entire body, from your toes to your neck, tightening a certain muscle group before releasing it.

9. Rub Vicks Vaporub on feet for congestion: To temporarily relieve a cough, try applying the mentholated topical cream on the soles of your feet and immediately covering with a pair of socks. There is no scientific explanation for why this old wives' trick works, but many stuffy nose-sufferers (and even nurses and doctors) swear by it.

10. Smile to make yourself happier: Scientists have found that the simple act of smiling can lower blood pressure and release stress, giving you an instant mood boost (yes, even forced smiles count!).

11. Press your tongue against the roof of your mouth to beat brain freeze: Also referred to as "ice cream headaches," brain freezes are caused by a rapid increase in blood flow to the brain. After you down a frozen treat, try thrusting your tongue against the roof of your mouth - this will warm up the palate and ease the flow of blood to the brain.

12. Use ginger to prevent motion sickness: Twenty minutes before travel, take two capsules of powdered ginger to ease an upset stomach caused by motion sickness.

13. Shake your head to wake up sleepy feet: It happens to all of us - you're sitting in an awkward position when all of a sudden your foot, hand or other body part falls asleep. To quickly eliminate that uncomfortable tingling sensation, move your head side to side. The movement helps relieve nerve tension.

14. Alleviate nausea by massaging wrist: Relieve nausea by lightly massaging the pressure point on the inside of your wrist, about three finger widths below the base of your palm.

15. Squeeze lemon to erase pimples: Banish breakouts by dabbing a little lemon juice on problem areas - its antibacterial properties will help kill excess bacteria and reduce acne.

16. Dab on clove oil to alleviate toothache pain: Apply a very small amount of clove oil to a cotton swab and gently dab onto the affected tooth area. The essential oil has been shown in studies to have analgesic and antibacterial properties, making it a useful tool in treating bacteria-caused toothaches.

17. Inhale onion vapors for sinus relief: Chop up an onion, put it in a bowl and inhale the onion fumes.

18. Stop mouth bleeds with tea bags: To stop mouth bleeds after oral surgery or injuries, apply a moistened tea bag to the affected area; the tannins in tea help the blood coagulate faster.

19. Steam to relieve nasal congestion: Steam helps to loosen mucus and clear out the sinus cavities, providing relief from nasal congestion. A hot bath works, too.

20. Sleep on your left side to prevent acid reflux: Researchers have determined that left side sleeping helps with digestion and eases heart burn pain.

☺ @ ☺

The Human Body

1. It's possible for your body to survive without a surprisingly large portion of its internal organs. Even if you lose your stomach, your spleen, 75% of your liver, 80% of your intestines, one kidney, one lung, and virtually every organ from your pelvic and groin area, you wouldn't be very healthy, but you would live.

2. During your lifetime, you will produce enough saliva to fill two swimming pools. Actually, Saliva is more important than you realise. If your saliva cannot dissolve something, you cannot taste it.

3. The largest cell in the human body is the female egg and the smallest is the male sperm. The egg is actually the only cell in the body that is visible with the naked eye.

4. The strongest muscle in the human body is the tongue and the hardest bone is the jawbone.

5. Human feet have 52 bones, accounting for one quarter of all the human body's bones.

6. Feet have 500,000 sweat glands and can produce more than a pint of sweat a day.

7. The acid in your stomach is strong enough to dissolve razor blades. The reason it doesn't eat away at your stomach is that the cells of your stomach wall renew themselves so frequently that you get a new stomach lining every three to four days.

8. The human lungs contain approximately 2,400 kilometres (1,500 mi) of airways and 300 to 500 million hollow cavities, having a total surface area of about 70 square meters, roughly the same area as one side of a tennis court. Furthermore, if all of the capillaries that surround the lung cavities were unwound and laid end to end, they would extend for about 992 kilometres. Also, your left lung is smaller than your right lung to make room for your heart.

9. Sneezes regularly exceed 150 kph, while coughs clock in at about 100 kph.

10. Your body gives off enough heat in 30 minutes to bring 3 litres of water to the boil.

11. Your body has enough iron in it to make a nail 3 inches long.

12. Earwax production is necessary for good ear health. It protects the delicate inner ear from bacteria, fungus, dirt and even insects. It also cleans and lubricates the ear canal.

13. Everyone has a unique smell, except for identical twins, who smell the same.

14. Your teeth start growing 6 months before you are born. This is why one out of every 2,000 new-born infants has a tooth when they are born.

15. A baby's head is one-quarter of its total length, but by the age of 25 will only be one-eighth of its total length. This is because people's heads grow at a much slower rate than the rest of their bodies.

16. Babies are born with 300 bones, but by adulthood the number is reduced to 206. Some of the bones, like skull bones, get fused into each other, bringing down the total number.

17. It's not possible to tickle yourself. This is because when you attempt to tickle yourself you are aware of the exact time and manner in which the tickling will occur, unlike when someone else tickles you.

18. Less than one third of the human race has 20-20 vision. This means that two out of three people cannot see perfectly.

19. Your nose can remember 50,000 different scents. But if you are a woman, you are a better smeller than men, and will remain a better smeller throughout your life.

20. The human body is estimated to have 60,000 miles of blood vessels.

21. The tooth is the only part of the human body that can't repair itself.

22. The three things pregnant women dream most of during their first trimester are frogs, worms and potted plants. Scientists have no idea why this is so, but attribute it to the growing imbalance of hormones in the body during pregnancy.

23. The life span of a human hair is 3 to 7 years on average. Every day the average person loses 60-100 strands of hair. But don't worry, you must lose over 50% of your scalp hairs before it is apparent to anyone.

24. The human brain cell can hold 5 times as much information as an encyclopaedia. Your brain uses 20% of the oxygen that enters your bloodstream, and is itself made up of 80% water. Though it interprets pain signals from the rest of the body, the brain itself cannot feel pain.

25. Your eyes are always the same size from birth but your nose and ears never stop growing.

26. By 60 years of age, 60% of men and 40% of women will snore.

27. We are about 1 cm taller in the morning than in the evening, because during normal activities during the day, the cartilage in our knees and other areas slowly compress.

28. The brain operates on the same amount of power as 10-watt light bulb, even while you are sleeping. In fact, the brain is much more active at night than during the day.

29. Nerve impulses to and from the brain travel as fast as 270 kilometres per hour. Neurons continue to grow throughout human life. Information travels at different speeds within different types of neurons .

30. It is a fact that people who dream more often and more vividly, on an average have a higher Intelligence Quotient.

31. The fastest growing nail is on the middle finger.

32. Facial hair grows faster than any other hair on the body. This is true for men as well as women.

33. There are as many hairs per square inch on your body as a chimpanzee.

34. A human foetus acquires fingerprints at the age of three months.

35. By the age of 60, most people will have lost about half their taste buds.

36. About 32 million bacteria call every inch of your skin home. But don't worry, a majority of these are harmless or even helpful bacteria.

37. The colder the room you sleep in, the higher the chances are that you'll have a bad dream.

38. Human lips have a reddish colour because of the great concentration of tiny capillaries just below the skin.

39. Three hundred million cells die in the human body every minute.

40. Like fingerprints, every individual has an unique tongue print that can be used for identification.

41. A human head remains conscious for about 15 to 20 seconds after it has been decapitated.

42. It takes 17 muscles to smile and 43 to frown.

43. Humans can make do longer without food than sleep. Provided there is water, the average human could survive a month to two months without food depending on their body fat and other factors.   Sleep deprived people, however, start experiencing radical personality and psychological changes after only a few sleepless days. The longest recorded time anyone has ever gone without sleep is 11 days, at the end of which the experimenter was awake, but stumbled over words, hallucinated and frequently forgot what he was doing.

44. The most common blood type in the world is Type O. The rarest blood type, A-H or Bombay blood, due to the location of its discovery, has been found in less than hundred people since it was discovered.

45. Every human spent about half an hour after being conceived, as a single cell. Shortly afterwards the cells begin rapidly dividing and begin forming the components of a tiny embryo.

46. Right-handed people live, on average, nine years longer than left-handed people do.

47. Your ears secrete more earwax when you are afraid than when you aren't.

48. Koalas and primates are the only animals with unique fingerprints.

49. Humans are the only animals to produce emotional tears.

50. The human heart creates enough pressure to squirt blood 8 metres in the air.

☺ @ ☺

Difference between Complete and Finished..

No dictionary has been able to adequately explain the difference between COMPLETE and FINISHED. However, in a recent linguistic conference held in London, England, and attended by some of the best linguists in the world: Samsundar Balgobin, a Guyanese, was the clear winner.

His final challenge was this: Some say there is no difference between COMPLETE and FINISHED. Please explain the difference between COMPLETE and FINISHED in a way that is easy to understand. Here is his astute answer:

"When you marry the right woman, you are COMPLETE. But, when you marry the wrong woman, you are FINISHED. And when the right one catches you with the wrong one, you are COMPLETELY FINISHED!"

The Robot

A father buys a lie-detector robot that slaps people when they lie.

He decides to test it out at dinner one night.
The father asks his son what he did that day.
The son says, "I did some homework." The robot slaps the son.
The son says, "OK, I was at a friend's house watching movies."
Dad asks, "What movie did you watch?"
Son says, "Toy Story." The robot slaps the son again.
Son says, "OK! OK! We were watching porn!"
Dad says, "What?? At your age I didn't even know what porn was!" The robot slaps the father.
Mum laughs and says, "Well, he certainly is your son!" The robot slaps the mother.

P.S. Robot for sale

☺   @   ☺

Shy Girl

A young girl started work in the village chemist shop. She was very shy about having to sell condoms to the public.

The owner was going on holiday for a couple of days and asked if she would be willing to run the shop on her own. She had to confide in him her worries about selling the contraceptives.

"Look," he said. "My regular customers don't ask for condoms, they'll ask for a 310 [small] a 320 [medium] or a 330 [large]. The word condom won't even be used.

The first day was fine but on the second day a guy came in to the shop, put out his hand and said "350".

The girl panicked. She phoned the owner on his mobile and told him of her predicament.

"Go back in and check if he has a yellow bucket hanging between his legs" her boss told her.

She peeped through the door and saw the yellow bucket hanging between his legs. "Yes "! She said "He's got one hanging there!"

The boss said "Go back in and give him £3.50, he's the window cleaner."

☺ @ ☺

Cell Phone Courtesy

After a tiring day, a commuter settled down in her seat and closed her eyes as the train rolled out of the station. As the train rolled out of the station, the guy sitting next to her pulled out his cell phone and started talking in a loud voice:

"Hi sweetheart. It's Eric. I'm on the train. Yes, I know it's the six thirty and not the four thirty, but I had a long meeting. No, honey, not with that blonde from the accounts office. With the boss. No sweetheart, you're the only one in my life. Yes, I'm sure, cross my heart!"

Fifteen minutes later, he was still talking loudly, when the young woman sitting next to him had had enough and leaned over and said into the phone, "Eric, turn that phone off and come back to bed."

Eric doesn't use his cell phone in public any longer.

☺ @ ☺

1981 & 2005 - Two Interesting Years

Interesting Year 1981

1. Prince Charles got married.
2. Liverpool crowned soccer Champions of Europe.
3. Australia lost the Ashes.
4.. The Pope died.

Interesting Year 2005

1. Prince Charles got married.
2. Liverpool crowned soccer Champions of Europe.
3. Australia lost the Ashes.
4. The Pope died.

Lesson to be learned:

The next time Charles gets married, someone should warn the Pope.

☺ @ ☺

Who Said Footballers Aren't Intelligent?

My parents have always been there for me, ever since I was about 7. "

David Beckham

"I would not be bothered if we lost every game as long as we won the league."

Mark Viduka

"Alex Ferguson is the best manager I've ever had at this level. Well, he's the only manager I've actually had at this level. But he's the best manager I've ever had."

David Beckham

"If you don't believe you can win, there is no point in getting out of bed at the end of the day."

Neville Southall

"I've had 14 bookings this season - 8 of which were my fault, but 7 of which were disputable."

Paul Gascoigne

"I've never wanted to leave. I'm here for the rest of my life, and hopefully after that as well."

Alan Shearer

"I'd like to play for an Italian club, like Barcelona "

Mark Draper

"You've got to believe that you're going to win, and I believe we'll win the World Cup until the final whistle blows and we're knocked out."

Peter Shilton

"I faxed a transfer request to the club at the beginning of the week, but let me state that I don't want to leave Leicester "

Stan Collymore

"I was watching the Blackburn game on TV on Sunday when it flashed on the screen that George (Ndah) had scored in the first minute at Birmingham .. My first reaction was to ring him up. Then I remembered he was out there playing."

Ade Akinbiyi

"Without being too harsh on David Beckham, he cost us the match."

Ian Wright

"I'm as happy as I can be - but I have been happier."

Ugo Ehiogu

"Leeds is a great club and it's been my home for years, even though I live in Middlesborough."
Jonathan Woodgate

"I can see the carrot at the end of the tunnel."
Stuart Pearce

"I took a whack on my left ankle, but something told me it was my right."
Lee Hendrie

"I couldn't settle in Italy - it was like living in a foreign country."
Ian Rush

" Germany are a very difficult team to play...they had 11 internationals out there today."
Steve Lomas

"I always used to put my right boot on first, and then obviously my right sock."
Barry Venison

"I definitely want Brooklyn to be christened, but I don't know into what religion yet."
David Beckham

"The Brazilians were South American, and the Ukrainians will be more European."
Phil Neville

"All that remains is for a few dots and commas to be crossed."
Mitchell Thomas

"One accusation you can't throw at me is that I've always done my best."
Alan Shearer

☺ @ ☺

CREATIVE LOGS
EXERCISE BLOCK / INSTRUCTIONS
1- PLACE BLOCK ON FLOOR IN CENTRE OF ROOM

2- WALK AROUND BLOCK TWICE,
SIT DOWN AND RELAX

3- IF ANYONE ASKS, HAVE YOU EXERCISED TODAY?
TELL THEM YOU WALKED AROUND THE BLOCK **TWICE!!!**

☺ @ ☺

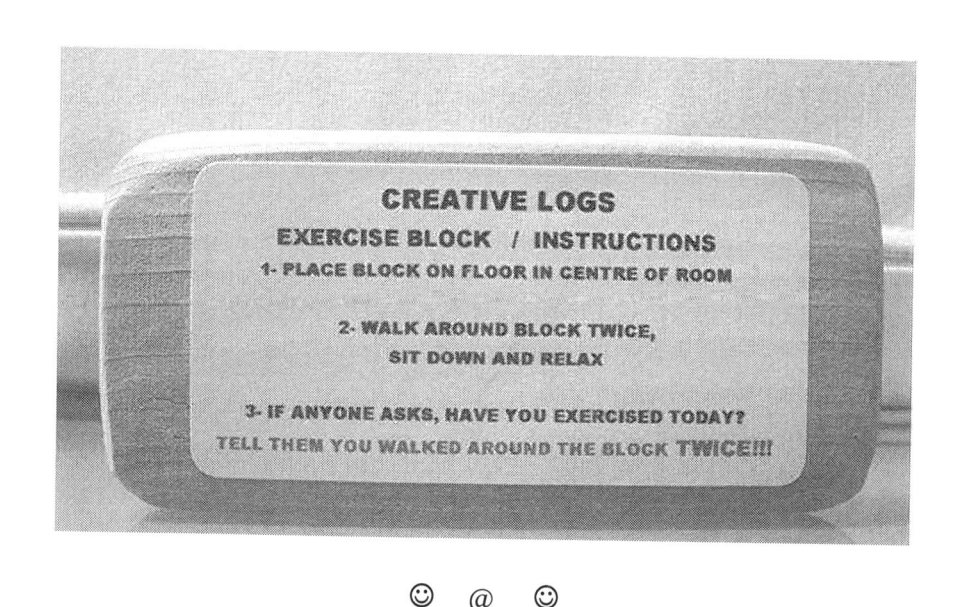

You don't have to be an engineer to appreciate this story.

A toothpaste factory had a problem: they sometimes shipped empty boxes, without the tube inside. This was due to the way the production line was set up, and people with experience in designing production lines will tell you how difficult it is to have everything happen with timings so precise that every single unit coming out of it is perfect 100% of the time. Small variations in the environment (which can't be controlled in a cost-effective fashion) mean you must have quality assurance checks smartly distributed across the line so that customers all the way down to the supermarket don't get mad and buy another brand instead.

Understanding how important that was, the CEO of the toothpaste factory got the top people in the company together and they decided to start a new project, in which they would hire an external engineering company to solve their empty boxes problem, as their engineering department was already too stretched to take on any extra effort.

The project followed the usual process: budget and project sponsor allocated, RFP, third-parties selected, and six months (and $8 million) later they had a fantastic solution - on time, on budget, high quality and everyone in the project had a great time. They solved the problem by using high-tech precision scales that would sound a bell and flash lights whenever a toothpaste box would weigh less than it should. The line would stop, and someone had to walk over and yank the defective box out of it, pressing another button when done to re-start the line.

A while later, the CEO decides to have a look at the ROI of the project: amazing results! No empty boxes ever shipped out of the factory after the scales were put in place. Very few customer complaints and they were gaining market share. "That's some money well spent!" - he says, before looking closely at the other statistics in the report.

It turns out; the number of defects picked up by the scales was 0 after three weeks of production use. It should've been picking up at least a dozen a day, so maybe there was something wrong with the report. He filed a bug against it, and after some investigation, the engineers come back saying the report was actually correct. The scales really weren't picking up any defects, because all boxes that got to that point in the conveyor belt were good.

Puzzled, the CEO travels down to the factory, and walks up to the part of the line where the precision scales were installed. A few feet before the scale, there was a $20 desk fan, blowing the empty boxes out of the belt and into a bin.

"Oh, that," says one of the workers -"one of the guys put it there 'cause he was tired of walking over..... 'every time the bell rang".

☺ @ ☺

The Barber

A guy stuck his head into a barbershop and asked, 'How long before I can get a haircut ?

The barber looked around the shop full of customers and said, 'About 2 hours.'

The guy left.

A few days later, the same guy stuck his head in the door and asked, 'How long before I can get a haircut?'

The barber looked around at the shop and said, 'About 3 hours.'

The guy left.

A week later, the same guy stuck his head in the shop and asked, 'How long before I can get a haircut?

The barber looked around the shop and said, 'About an hour and a half.'

The guy left.

The barber turned to his friend and said, 'Hey, Bob, do me a favour. Follow him and see where he goes. He keeps asking how long he has to wait for a haircut, but he never comes back.'

A little while later, Bob returned to the shop, laughing hysterically.

The barber asked, 'So, where does he go when he leaves ?'

Bob looked up, wiped the tears from his eyes and said, 'Your house!'

☺ @ ☺

Brain Study....

I've seen this with the letters out of order, but this is the first time I've seen it with numbers.

Good example of a Brain Study: If you can read this you have a strong mind:

>7H15 M3554G3
>53RV35 7O PR0V3
>H0W 0UR M1ND5 C4N
>D0 4M4Z1NG 7H1NG5!
>1MPR3551V3 7H1NG5!
>1N 7H3 B3G1NN1NG
>17 WA5 H4RD BU7
>N0W, 0N 7H15 LIN3
>Y0UR M1ND 1S
>R34D1NG 17
>4U70M471C4LLY
>W17H 0U7 3V3N
>7H1NK1NG 4B0U7 17,
>B3 PROUD! 0NLY
>C3R741N P30PL3 C4N
>R3AD 7H15.
>PL3453 F0RW4RD 1F
>U C4N R34D 7H15.

☺ @ ☺

British Hospitality

An American tourist in London decides to skip his tour group and explore the city on his own. He wanders around, seeing the sights, and occasionally stopping at a quaint pub to soak up the local culture, chat with the lads, and have a pint of Guinness.

After a while, he finds himself in a very high class neighbourhood.....big, stately residences... no pubs, no stores, no restaurants, and worst of all...

NO PUBLIC TOILETS.

He really, really has to go, after all those Guinness's. He finds a narrow side street, with high walls surrounding the adjacent buildings and decides to use the wall to solve his problem. As he is unzipping, he is tapped on the shoulder by a London Bobby, who says, "I say, sir, you simply cannot do that here, you know."

"I'm very sorry, officer," replies the American, "but I really, really HAVE TO GO, and I just can't find a public toilet."

"Ah, yes," said the bobby..."Just follow me". He leads him to a back "delivery alley", then along a wall to a gate, which he opens. "In there," points the bobby. "Whiz away sir, anywhere you want."

The fellow enters and finds himself in the most beautiful garden he has ever seen.

Manicured grass lawns, statuary, fountains, sculpted hedges, and huge beds of gorgeous flowers, all in perfect bloom. Since he has the copper's blessing, he unburdens himself and is greatly relieved.

As he goes back through the gate, he says to the bobby, "That was really decent of you... is that what you call 'English Hospitality'?"

"No, sir" replies the bobby, "that is what we call the French Embassy."

☺ @ ☺

Ryanair

Spare a thought for Michael O'Leary, Chief Executive of 'Ryanair'.......

Arriving in a hotel in Dublin, he went to the bar and asked for a pint of draught Guinness. The barman nodded and said, "That will be one Euro please, Mr. O'Leary."

Somewhat taken aback, O'Leary replied, "That's very cheap," and handed over his money

"Well, we try to stay ahead of the competition", said the barman. "And we are serving free pints every Wednesday evening from 6 until 8. We have the cheapest beer in Ireland"

"That is remarkable value" Michael comments

"I see you don't seem to have your own glass" said the barman, "so you'll probably need one of ours. That will be 3 euros please."

O'Leary scowled, but paid up. He took his drink and walked towards a seat. "Ah, you want to sit down?" said the barman. "That'll be an extra 2 euro.- You could have pre-book the seat, and it would have only cost you a Euro."

"I think you may to be too big for the seat sir, can I ask you to sit in this frame please"

Michael attempts to sit down but the frame is too small and when he can't squeeze in he complains "Nobody would fit in that little frame".

"I'm afraid if you can't fit in the frame you'll have to pay an extra surcharge of 4 euro for your seat sir"

O'Leary swore to himself, but paid up. "I see that you have brought your laptop with you" added the barman. "And since that wasn't pre-booked either, that will be another 3 euro."

O'Leary was so annoyed that he walked back to the bar, slammed his drink on the counter, and yelled, "This is ridiculous, I want to speak to the manager".

"Ah, I see you want to use the counter," says the barman, "that will be 2 euro please." O'Leary's face was red with rage.

"Do you know who I am?"

"Of course I do Mr. O'Leary,"

"I've had enough, What sort of hotel is this? I come in for a quiet drink and you treat me like this. I insist on speaking to a manager!"

"Here is his E mail address, or if you wish, you can contact him between 9 and 9.10 every morning, Monday to Tuesday at this free phone number. Calls are free, until they are answered, then there is a talking charge of only 10 cents per second"

"I will never use this bar again"

"OK sir, but remember, we are the only hotel in Ireland selling pints for one Euro".

☺ @ ☺

Costa . . .

A man rang the Airfix Model shop and asked, "Do you have a model of an Italian cruise liner?" The shop owner said, "Yes". The man said, "Brilliant! Can you put it on one side for me please".

Answers of a Student who Obtained 0%

I simply think this person is misunderstood. He will one day be a politician! Probably a future Prime minister?

Q1. In which battle did Napoleon die?
* his last battle

Q2. Where was the Declaration of Independence signed?
* at the bottom of the page

Q3. River Ravi flows in which state?
* liquid

Q4. What is the main reason for divorce?
* marriage

Q5. What is the main reason for failure?
* exams

Q6. What can you never eat for breakfast?
* Lunch & dinner

Q7. What looks like half an apple?
* The other half

Q8. If you throw a red stone into the blue sea what it will become?
* it will simply become wet

Q9. How can a man go eight days without sleeping?
* No problem, he sleeps at night.

Q10. How can you lift an elephant with one hand?
* You will never find an elephant that has only one hand..

Q11. If you had three apples and four oranges in one hand and four apples and three oranges in other hand, what would you have ?
* Very large hands

Q12. If it took eight men ten hours to build a wall, how long would it take four men to build it?
* No time at all, the wall is already built.

Q13. How can you drop a raw egg onto a concrete floor without cracking it?
*Concrete floors are very hard to crack.

☺ @ ☺

Milk and Eggs

This is a story which is perfectly logical to all males:

A wife asks her husband, "Could you please go shopping for me and buy one carton of milk, and if they have eggs, get 6."

A short time later the husband comes back with 6 cartons of milk. The wife asks him, "Why did you buy 6 cartons of milk?"

He replied, "They had eggs."

☺ @ ☺

Suffer Little Children . . .

I was sitting on a bus behind a mother and her young son. Her boy kept looking around and making weird funny faces at me. After a few minutes I tired of his antics so I said, "When I was a young boy my mother told me that if I made an ugly face it just might stay that way."
The little swine replied, "Well, you can't say you weren't warned."

Amazing, Simple Home Remedies:

1. Avoid cutting yourself when slicing vegetables by getting someone else to hold the vegetables while you chop.

2. Avoid arguments with the females about lifting the toilet seat by using the sink.

3. For high blood pressure sufferers ~ simply cut yourself and bleed for a few minutes, thus reducing the pressure on your veins. Remember to use a timer.

4. A mousetrap placed on top of your alarm clock will prevent you from rolling over and going back to sleep after you hit the snooze button.

5. If you have a bad cough, take a large dose of laxatives. Then you won't dare to cough.

6. You need only two tools in life - WD-40 And duct tape. If it doesn't move but should, use the WD-40. If it shouldn't move but does, use the duct tape.

7. If you can't fix it with a hammer, you've got an electrical problem.

☺ @ ☺

Why We Love Children

   I was driving with my three young children one warm summer evening when a woman in the convertible ahead of us stood up and waved. She was stark naked! As I was reeling from the shock, I heard my 5-year-old shout from the back seat, 'Mum, that lady isn't wearing a seat belt!'

On the first day of school, a first-grader handed his teacher a note from his mother. The note read, 'The opinions expressed by this child are not necessarily those of his parents.'

A mother was trying hard to get the ketchup out of the jar. During her struggle the phone rang so she asked her 4-year-old daughter to answer the phone. 'Mummy can't come to the phone to talk to you right now. She's hitting the bottle.'

A little boy got lost at the YMCA and found himself in the women's locker room. When he was spotted, the room burst into shrieks, with ladies grabbing towels and running for cover. The little boy watched in amazement and then asked, 'What's the matter, haven't you ever seen a little boy before?'

While taking a routine vandalism report at a primary school, I was interrupted by a little girl about 6 years old. Looking up and down at my uniform, she asked, 'Are you a policeman?' 'Yes,' I answered and continued writing the report. My mother said if I ever needed
help I should ask the police. Is that right?' 'Yes, that's right,' I told her. 'Well, then,' she said as she extended her foot toward me, 'would you please tie my shoelace?'

It was the end of the day when I parked my police van in front of the station. As I gathered my equipment, my K-9 partner, Jake, was barking, and I saw a little boy staring in at me. 'Is that a dog you have in your van ?' he asked. 'It sure is,' I replied. Puzzled, the boy looked at me and then towards the back of the van. Finally he said, 'What did he do?'

A little girl was watching her parents dress for a party. When she saw her dad donning his DJ, she warned, 'Daddy, you shouldn't wear that suit.'
'And why not, darling?'
'You know that it always gives you a headache the next morning.'

While working for an organization that delivers lunches to elderly housebound, I used to take my 4 year-old daughter on my afternoon rounds. She was unfailingly intrigued by the various appliances of old age, particularly the canes, walkers and wheelchairs. One day I found her staring at a pair of false teeth soaking in a glass. As I braced myself for the inevitable barrage of questions, she merely turned and whispered, 'The tooth fairy will never believe this!'

A little girl had just finished her first week of school. 'I'm just wasting my time,' she said to her mother. 'I can't read, I can't write, and they won't let me talk!'

A little boy opened the big family Bible. He was fascinated as he fingered through the old pages. Suddenly, something fell out of the Bible. He picked up the object and looked at it. What he saw was an old leaf that had been pressed in between the pages. 'Mummy, look what I found,' the boy called out.
'What have you got there, dear?'
With astonishment in the young boy's voice, he answered, 'I think it's Adam's underwear!'

☺ @ ☺

Perspective

An American investment banker was sitting on the jetty of a small coastal Mexican village when a fisherman came in to dock in his little boat.

Lying in the bottom of the boat were several large yellow fin tuna. The American complimented the fisherman on his fish and asked how long it took to catch them.

The fisherman replied, "Just a little time."

The American then asked, "Why didn't you stay out longer and catch more fish?"

The fisherman said, "With this I have more than enough to support my family's needs."

The American asked, "But what do you do with the rest of your time?"

The fisherman said, "I sleep late, I fish a little, I play with my children, I take siesta with my wife, Maria, and I stroll into the village each evening where I sip wine and play guitar with my amigos."

"Look," said the American, "I'm an investment banker and I think I could help you."

"How is that?" the fisherman asked

"Well," said the American, "You can spend more time fishing and you can sell the extra fish. With the profits you could buy a bigger boat and catch even more fish. With the extra profit from the bigger boat you could buy several boats. Eventually you would have a fleet of fishing boats. Instead of selling your fish to a middleman you would sell directly to the processor. Eventually you could open your own processing factory. You would control the product, processing and distribution. You'd leave this tiny place and move to Mexico City, then to Los Angeles and eventually to New York where you would run your ever-expanding fishing empire."

The fisherman asked, "How long will this take?"

"Twenty to twenty five years," the American replied.

"And what would I do then?" asked the fisherman.

The American laughed and said "That's the best part. When the time is right you would sell your company to the public and become very rich. You'd be worth millions."

"Millions? Then what?" asked the fisherman.

The American said, "Then you could retire from the rat race. You could move to one of these little villages on the Mexican coast where you could sleep late, fish a little, play with your kids, take siesta with your wife, stroll to the village in the evenings where you could sip wine and play your guitar with your amigos. It would be like living in paradise."

☺ @ ☺

Romance

An elderly couple had just learned how to send text messages on their cell phones. The wife was a romantic type and the husband was more of a no-nonsense guy.

One afternoon the wife went out to meet a friend for coffee. She decided to send her husband a romantic text message and she wrote:

"If you are sleeping, send me your dreams.
If you are laughing, send me your smile.
If you are eating, send me a bite.
If you are drinking, send me a sip.
If you are crying, send me your tears.
I love you."
The husband texted back to her: "I'm on the toilet. Please advise."

☺ @ ☺

Sex After Surgery

A recent article in the Kentucky Post reported that a woman, one Anne Maynard, has sued St Luke's hospital, saying that after her husband had surgery there, he lost all interest in sex. A hospital spokesman replied ... "Mr. Maynard was admitted to Ophthalmology – all we did was correct his eyesight."

Children writing about the ocean

The next time you take an oceanography course you will be totally prepared.

1) - This is a picture of an octopus. It has eight testicles.
(Kelly, age 6)

2) - Oysters' balls are called pearls.
(Jerry, age 6)

3) - If you are surrounded by ocean, you are an island. If you don't have ocean all round you, you are incontinent.
(Mike, age 7)

4) - Sharks are ugly and mean, and have big teeth, just like Emily Richardson . She's not my friend any more.
(Kylie, age 6)

5) - A dolphin breaths through an asshole on the top of its head.
(Billy, age 8)

6) - My uncle goes out in his boat with 2 other men and a woman and pots and comes back with crabs.
(Millie, age 6)

7) - When ships had sails, they used to use the trade winds to cross the ocean. Sometimes when the wind didn't blow the sailors would whistle to make the wind come. My brother said they would have been better off eating beans.
(William, age 7)

8) - Mermaids live in the ocean. I like mermaids. They are beautiful and I like their shiny tails, but how on earth do mermaids get pregnant? Like, really?
(Helen, age 6)

9) - When you go swimming in the ocean, it is very cold, and it makes my willy small.
(Kevin, age 6)

10) - I'm not going to write about the ocean. My baby brother is always crying, my Dad keeps yelling at my Mom, and my big sister has just got pregnant, so I can't think what to write.

(Amy, age 6)

11) - Some fish are dangerous. Jellyfish can sting. Electric eels can give you a shock. They have to live in caves under the sea where I think they have to plug themselves in to chargers.

(Christopher, age 7)

12) - Divers have to be safe when they go under the water. Divers can't go down alone, so they have to go down on each other.

(Becky, age 8)

13) - On vacation my Mum went water skiing. She fell off when she was going very fast. She says she won't do it again because water fired right up her big fat ass.

(Julie, age 7)

14) - The ocean is made up of water and fish. Why the fish don't drown I don't know..

(Bobby, age 6)

15) - My dad was a sailor on the ocean. He knows all about the ocean. What he doesn't know is why he quit being a sailor and married my mum.

(James, age 7)

☺ @ ☺

Concealing The Profession

A young man and his date were parked on a back road some distance from town. They were about to have sex when the girl stopped.

"I really should have mentioned this earlier, but I'm actually a hooker and I charge $20 for sex." The man reluctantly paid her, and they did their thing.

After a cigarette, the man just sat in the driver's seat looking out the window. "Why aren't we going anywhere?" asked the girl.

"Well, I should have mentioned this before, but I'm actually a taxi driver, and the fare back to town is $25..."

☺ @ ☺

So – Which way is the Car Going?

☺ @ ☺

In church I heard a lady in the pew next to me saying a prayer. It was so sweet and sincere that I just had to share with you..

Dear Lord,
This has been a tough two or three years.
You have taken my favourite actor Patrick Swayze.
My favourite musician Michael Jackson.
My favourite Blues Singer Amy Winehouse.
My favourite actress Elizabeth Taylor.
And now my favourite singer Whitney Houston.
I just wanted you to know that my favourite politicians are Ed Miliband, Nick Clegg and Ed Balls.

☺ @ ☺

Only in the good old USA

This took place in Charlotte, North Carolina.
A lawyer purchased a box of very rare and expensive cigars, then insured them against, among other things...fire.
Within a month, having smoked his entire stockpile of these great cigars, the lawyer filed a claim against the insurance company .In his claim, the lawyer stated the cigars were lost 'in a series of small fires.'

The insurance company refused to pay, citing the obvious reason, that the man had consumed the cigars in the normal fashion.

The lawyer sued - and WON! (Stay with me.)

Delivering the ruling, the judge agreed with the insurance company that the claim was frivolous. The judge stated nevertheless, that the lawyer held a policy from the company, in which it had warranted that the cigars were insurable and also guaranteed that it would insure them against fire, without defining what is considered to be unacceptable 'fire' and was obligated to pay the claim.

Rather than endure lengthy and costly appeal process, the insurance company accepted the ruling and paid $15,000 to the lawyer for his loss of the cigars that perished in the 'fires'.

NOW FOR THE BEST PART...
After the lawyer cashed the check, the insurance company had him arrested on 24 counts of ARSON! With his own insurance claim and testimony from the previous case being used against him, the lawyer was convicted of intentionally burning his insured property and was sentenced to 24 months in jail and a $24,000 fine.

This true story won First Place in last year's Criminal Lawyers Award contest.

Puns Upon A Time

An Englishman's home is his castle, in a manor of speaking.
Dijon vu - the same mustard as before.
Practice safe eating - always use condiments.
Shotgun wedding - A case of wife or death.
A man needs a mistress just to break the monogamy.
A hangover is the wrath of grapes.
Dancing cheek-to-cheek is really a form of floor play.
Does the name Pavlov ring a bell?
Reading while sunbathing makes you well red.
When two egotists meet, it's an I for an I.
A bicycle can't stand on its own because it is two tired.
What's the definition of a will? (It's a dead give away.)
Time flies like an arrow. Fruit flies like a banana.
In democracy your vote counts. In feudalism your count votes.
She was engaged to a boyfriend with a wooden leg but broke it off.
A chicken crossing the road is poultry in motion.
If you don't pay your exorcist, you get repossessed.
With her marriage, she got a new name and a dress.
The man who fell into an upholstery machine is fully recovered.
You feel stuck with your debt if you can't budge it.
Local Area Network in Australia : the LAN down under.
Every calendar's days are numbered.
A lot of money is tainted - Taint yours and taint mine.
A boiled egg in the morning is hard to beat.
He had a photographic memory that was never developed.
A midget fortune-teller who escapes from prison is a small medium at large.
Once you've seen one shopping centre, you've seen a mall.
Bakers trade bread recipes on a knead-to-know basis.
Santa's helpers are subordinate clauses.
Acupuncture is a jab well done.

☺ @ ☺

An Obituary printed in the Times - Interesting and sadly rather true.

Today we mourn the passing of a beloved old friend, Common Sense, who has been with us for many years. No one knows for sure how old he was, since his birth records were long ago lost in bureaucratic red tape. He will be remembered as having cultivated such valuable lessons as:
- Knowing when to come in out of the rain;
- Why the early bird gets the worm;
- Life isn't always fair;
- and maybe it was my fault.

Common Sense lived by simple, sound financial policies (don't spend more than you can earn) and reliable strategies (adults, not children, are in charge).

His health began to deteriorate rapidly when well-intentioned but overbearing regulations were set in place. Reports of a 6-year-old boy charged with sexual harassment for kissing a classmate; teens suspended from school for using mouthwash after lunch; and a teacher fired for reprimanding an unruly student, only worsened his condition.

Common Sense lost ground when parents attacked teachers for doing the job that they themselves had failed to do in disciplining their unruly children.

It declined even further when schools were required to get parental consent to administer sun lotion or an aspirin to a student; but could not inform parents when a student became pregnant and wanted to have an abortion..

Common Sense lost the will to live as the churches became businesses; and criminals received better treatment than their victims.

Common Sense took a beating when you couldn't defend yourself from a burglar in your own home and the burglar could sue you for assault.

Common Sense finally gave up the will to live, after a woman failed to realize that a steaming cup of coffee was hot. She spilled a little in her lap, and was promptly awarded a huge settlement.

Common Sense was preceded in death, by his parents, Truth and Trust, by his wife, Discretion, by his daughter, Responsibility, and by his son, Reason.

He is survived by his 4 stepbrothers;
I Know My Rights
I Want It Now
Someone Else Is To Blame
I'm A Victim

Not many attended his funeral because so few realized he was gone.

☺   @   ☺

Police Harassment Explained

Recently, the Chula Vista Police Department ran an e-mail forum (a question and answer exchange) with the topic being,"Community Policing." One of the civilian email participants posed the following question,

 "I would like to know how it is possible for police officers to continually harass people and get away with it?"

From the "other side" (the law enforcement side) Sgt. Bennett, obviously a cop with a sense of humor replied:

"First of all, let me tell you this...it's not easy. In Chula Vista, we average one cop for every 600 people. Only about 60% of those cops are on general duty (or what you might refer to as "patrol") where we do most of our harassing.

The rest are in non-harassing departments that do not allow them contact with the day to day innocents. And at any given moment, only one-fifth of the 60% of patrollers are on duty and available for harassing people while the rest are off duty. So roughly, one cop is responsible for harassing about 5,000 residents.

When you toss in the commercial business, and tourist locations that attract people from other areas, sometimes you have a situation where a single cop is responsible for harassing 10,000 or more people a day.

Now, your average ten-hour shift runs 36,000 seconds long. This gives a cop one second to harass a person, and then only three-fourths of a second to eat a doughnut AND then find a new person to harass. This is not an easy task. To be honest, most cops are not up to this challenge day in and day out. It is just too tiring. What we do is utilize some tools to help us narrow down those people which we can realistically harass.

The tools available to us are as follows:

PHONE: People will call us up and point out things that cause us to focus on a person for special harassment. "My neighbour is beating his wife" is a code phrase used often. This means we'll come out and give somebody some special harassment.

Another popular one is, "There's a guy breaking into a house." The harassment team is then put into action.

CARS: We have special cops assigned to harass people who drive. They like to harass the drivers of fast cars, cars with no insurance or no driver's licenses.

It's lots of fun when you pick them out of traffic for nothing more obvious than running a red light. Sometimes you get to really heap the harassment on when you find they have drugs in the car, they are drunk, or have an outstanding warrant on file.

RUNNERS: Some people take off running just at the sight of a police officer. Nothing is quite as satisfying as running after them like a beagle on the scent of a bunny. When you catch them you can harass them for hours.

STATUTES: When we don't have PHONES or CARS and have nothing better to do, there are actually books that give us ideas for reasons to harass folks. They are called "Statutes"; Criminal Codes, Motor Vehicle Codes, etc... They all spell out all sorts of things for which you can really mess with people.

After you read the statute, you can just drive around for awhile until you find someone violating one of these listed offences and harass them. Just last week I saw a guy trying to steal a car. Well, there's this book we have that says that's not allowed. That meant I got permission to harass this guy. It is a really cool system that we have set up, and it works pretty well.

We seem to have a never-ending supply of folks to harass. And we get away with it. Why? Because for the good citizens who pay the tab, we try to keep the streets safe for them, and they pay us to "harass" some people.

Next time you are in my town, give me the old "single finger wave." That's another one of those codes. It means, "You can harass me." It's one of our favourites.

☺ @ ☺

Light travels faster than sound. This is why some people appear bright until you hear them speak.

☺ @ ☺

Some After Dinner Gems

Colonel D.J.Dean, V.C., O.B.E., T.D., D.L., J.P.,
Deputy Lieutenant of Kent, 1957.

When a young lieutenant was promoted to captain, by error the date in the "Gazette" appeared as April 1st, 1041, instead of 1941. That evening, after celebrating his promotion in the Mess with his fellow officers, they persuaded him to apply for back pay and allowances. The application was correctly made out, quoting Pay warrant and King's Regulations, and was posted. Then all retired to bed.

Next morning the young officer realized with horror what he had done and was filled with trepidation as to the outcome. A Court Martial?

Weeks later the Paymaster replied: "Your application for pay and allowances dating back to April 1st, 1041 has been found to be in order and your account has accordingly been credited with £39,999. You appear however to have overlooked a paragraph in King's Regulations under which a Commanding Officer is personally responsible for any guns or horses lost in action owing to negligence. If the C.O. is killed his responsibility devolves upon the next senior surviving officer. Your letter proves conclusively that you are the sole survivor of the Battle of Hastings (1066 A.D.) where 20,000 horses valued at £2 each were lost by negligence. The responsibility for £40,000 therefore falls upon you. I have accordingly adjusted you account to the extent of a net debit of £1."

"What kind of sport has our distinguished guest had?" Lord Minto, one time Viceroy of India, asked the native bearer, who had attended an American guest.
"Oh," replied the Indian, "the young sahib shot divinely but Allah was merciful to the birds."

Lord Delfont,
Chairman & Chief Executive of Trusthouse Forte Leisure Ltd.

The scene is a monastery where every seven years a monk is selected to pass an opinion of life within the community.
At one of the seven year meeting, the Abbot calls upon Brother Albert to say what he feels, and the privileged monk asks: "Why is our soup always cold?"

Seven years later, Brother John is invited to speak, and he says: "The soup is not always cold but is sometimes hot."

Another seven years pass and this time Brother Richard is called upon. He says: "I want to resign the Order."

When asked why, he contends: "I'm sick and tired of this constant bickering."

The Suffragan Bishop of Dorking
(The Rt. Rev. Kenneth Dawson Evans).

It is said that Frederick Temple, Archbishop of Canterbury eighty years ago, was much feared. This was particularly the case when he entertained at his house those who were about to be ordained. It was the interview that they feared.

He said to one young man who was to be ordained deacon on the following day. "I will lie on the couch, as if I were ill. Go out, come in again and 'sick visit' me."

The young man went out, knocked at the door, walked up to the Most Reverend, Frederick, Lord Archbishop of Canterbury, looked at him with a serious air, waggled his finger and said: "Freddie, You're on the drink again!"

Judge The Lord Dunboyne.

A schoolmaster who tried to teach me divinity went on holiday in the Holy Land, and took a trip on the Sea of Galilee for which he was in his view overcharged. He paid ... and as an afterthought, gently remarked:
"No wonder Jesus walked."

Sir Kingsley Dunham, F.R.S.,
Foreign Secretary, The Royal Society, 1971-76; Former Director, Institute of Geological Science.
I was at the Chicago World's Fair of 1933 as a young man. Finding a stand making phonograph recordings, I decided to send one to my fiancée (now Lady Dunham) and went into the studio to dictate a long message in what were, to say the least, very endearing terms.

Looking through the glass windows I noticed a small crowd had gathered outside. When I went out, armed with my record, I found out why; the whole proceedings had been relayed on powerful loudspeakers.

"My," someone remarked, "it sure was nice to hear a genuine English voice."

Sir Esmond Durlacher
Member of The Stock Exchange, 1926-77.
Amongst the majority of the racing public it has always been the view that the chief obstacle to their making money is the bookmaker. He pinches the odds and whatever happens, he always manages to make a profit. In the City, those who deal in stocks and shares – the speculators, the stockbrokers, the investment managers of the insurance companies, the pension funds, the unit trusts, etc. etc. – also hold very much the same view of the stock jobbers! In fact, this has been so since Samuel Johnson described the stock-jobbing fraternity as "an unnecessary collection of low fellows who speculate in the 'Funds' and are of no benefit to anyone but themselves".

Wherefore the following story with the knowledge of the foregoing factors mentioned in this prologue is, I think, a good example of the ready wit of the members of the Stock Exchange.

One morning I was sitting at my desk when a friend – a member – rang me up and said he was sorry to hear our office had been burgled overnight, but had I heard the story (9.30 am) already circulating on the floor of the House. When I said:

"No I have not," he replied:

"It is understood that the burglars were very lucky and got away with only a small loss!!"   (And we had in fact been burgled!)

The Late Sir Cyril Dyson, President of the National Association of Goldsmiths in Great Britain and Iceland, 1957-70.

I was asked to present the prizes at a girls school; It is always difficult to think of something to say other than, "Congratulations", "Well done." Etc. The girls came up in age groups and eventually the head girl came up to collect the several prizes she had won. She was a nice looking girl of about 17, I wondered what I could say to her. Suddenly I thought that as this was her last term it would be appropriate to ask her: "And what are you going to do when you leave school?" she looked at me very coyly and said: "Well I had thought of going straight home."

Air Marshall Sir Thomas Elmhirst, K.B.E., C.B., A.F.C., Lieutenant Governor and Commander–in-chief of Guernsey,1953-58.

Scene: The small mail steamer from Glasgow on its route up the West coast of Scotland.
On the bridge the captain and a couple of lady schoolteachers he had invited up there.

A heavy shower of rain approaches. Captain in a loud voice down the "Voice pipe" to the saloon below where one of his crew is in charge of the bar: "Is there a big mackintosh down there that would cover two ladies?"

Reply, by a small man in the corner, after a moment's silence: "Noo, but there is a wee MacGregor here that is prepared to try."

Sir Basil Engholm, K.C.B.,
Permanent Secretary, Ministry of Agriculture and Fisheries, 1968-72.

A duke, living on his country estate, used to have his breakfast in bed every Sunday morning. One Sunday there was a knock at the door and a new very pretty young girl brought in his breakfast, and put it down on the bedside table.
"You're new, my dear," said the duke. "And where might you be from?
"From the village, sir," she said.
"Come and talk to me, my dear," said the duke.
"yes, sir," said the girl.
"You know, you're very pretty dear. Come and sit down on the bed," said the duke, patting a place near him.
"Yes, sir." Said the girl and came and sat down.
"You know my dear, you must learn the right way to address me. You should say "Your Grace"."
And the girl fell on her knees beside the bed, and said:
"For what I am about to receive, may the Lord make me truly thankful.

Lord Erskine of Rerrick, G.B.E., K.St.J., F.R.S.E., Hon. F.R.C.P.E., D.L., J.P.,   Governor of Northern Ireland, 1964-68.

Incident narrated to me by the late Rt. Hon. Thomas Johnston, C.H., which came to his knowledge while he was Regional Commissioner for Scotland during the war.

Air raid warden on his rounds in a populous and dark area of Glasgow observed a light which he went to investigate. The following conversation took place between him and a small boy who answered his knock on the door.
Warden: "Is your father in?"
Boy: "No, my father went oot when my mither came in."
Warden: "Is your mother in?"
Boy: "No, my mither went oot when my brither came in."
Warden: "Is your brother in?"
Boy: "No, my brither went oot when I came in."
Warden: "Then are you in charge of the house?"
Boy: "It's no a hoose, It's a lavatory!"

Sir George Erskine, C.B.E., Director, Morgan Grenfell & co., 1945-67
President, Institute of Bankers, 1954-56; High Sheriff of Surrey '63-64.

Australian on his cattle station when asked by a Scotsman if there were many Scottish people in Australia answered: "Yes, a good many but our real plague is rabbits."

☺ @ ☺

Religion

A young couple wanted to join the church, the vicar told them, 'We have a special requirement for new member couples. You must abstain from sex for one whole month.'

The couple agreed, but after two-and-a-half weeks returned to the Church. When the vicar ushered them into his office, the wife was crying and the husband was obviously very depressed.

'You are back so soon...Is there a problem?' the vicar inquired.

'We are terribly ashamed to admit that we did not manage to abstain from sex for the required month.' The young man replied sadly.

The vicar asked him what happened.

'Well, the first week was difficult... However, we managed to abstain through sheer willpower. The second week was terrible, but with the use of prayer, we managed to abstain. However, the third week was unbearable. We tried cold showers, Prayer, reading from the Bible....anything to keep our minds off Carnal Thoughts.

One afternoon my wife reached for a can of paint and dropped it. When she bent over to pick it up, I was overcome with lust and I just had my way with her right then and there. It was lustful, loud, passionate sex. It lasted for over an hour and when we were done we were both drenched in sweat,' admitted the man, shamefacedly.

The vicar lowered his head and said sternly, 'You understand this means you will not be welcome in our church.'

'We know.' said the young man, hanging his head, 'We're not welcome at Homebase either.

☺   @   ☺

How True is This?

Two different surgeries

Two patients limp into two different medical clinics with the same complaint. Both have trouble walking.

The FIRST patient is examined within the hour, is x-rayed the same day and has a time booked for surgery the following week.

The SECOND sees his family doctor after waiting a week for an appointment, then waits 8 weeks to see a specialist, who books an x-ray the following week, which isn't reviewed for another week and finally has his surgery scheduled for 6 months from then.

Why the different treatment for the two patients?

The FIRST is a Golden Retriever.
The SECOND is a Senior Citizen.

Next time take me to a vet!

☺ @ ☺

Welsh Rugby

Two 90 year old Welshmen, Dai and Emrys, have been friends all of their lives.

When it's clear that Emrys is dying, Dai visits him every day. One day Dai says, 'Emrys, we both loved rugby all our lives, and we played rugby on Saturdays together for so many years. Please do me one favour, when you get to Heaven, somehow you must let me know if there's rugby there.'

Emrys looks up at Dai from his death bed,' Dai, you've been my best friend for many years. If it's at all possible, I'll do this favour for you.

Shortly after that, Emrys passes on. At midnight a couple of nights later, Dai is awakened from a sound sleep by a blinding flash of white light and a voice calling out to him, 'Dai--Dai.'

'Who is it? Asks Dai sitting up suddenly. 'Who is it?'

'Dai--it's me, Emrys.'

'You're not Emrys. Emrys just died.'

'I'm telling you, it's me, Emrys,' insists the voice.'

'Emrys! Where are you?'

'In heaven', replies Emrys. 'I have some really good news and a little bad news.'

'Tell me the good news first,' says Dai.

The good news,' Emrys says,' is that there's rugby in heaven. Better yet, all of our old friends who died before us are here, too. Better than that, we're all young again. Better still, it's always spring time and it never rains or snows. And best of all, we can play rugby all we want, and we never get tired.'

'That's fantastic,' says Dai. 'It's beyond my wildest dreams! So what's the bad news?'

'You're in the team for Tuesday.'

☺   @   ☺

Mexican Maid

The Mexican maid asks for a pay increase.
 The wife was very upset about this and decided to talk to her about the raise.
 She asked: 'Now Maria, why do you want a pay increase?'
 Maria: 'Well, Señora, there are three reasons why I wanna increase. The first is that I iron better than you.'
 Wife: 'Who said you iron better than me?'
 Maria: 'Jor husban' say so.'
 Wife: 'Oh.'
 Maria: 'The second reason is that I am a better cook than you.'
 Wife: 'Nonsense, who said you were a better cook than me?'

Maria: 'Jor husban' did.'
Wife: 'Oh..'
Maria: 'The third reason is that I am better than you in bed.'
Wife: (really furious now) 'Did my husband say that as well?'
Maria: 'No Señora...the gardener did.'
Wife: 'So how much do you want?'

☺   @   ☺

How things really work

Three contractors are bidding to fix a broken wall at 10 Downing Street ; one from London , another from Bristol and the third, Liverpool .

They go with a government official to examine the wall.

The London contractor takes out a tape measure and does some measuring, then works some figures with a pencil.

'Well', he says, 'I figure the job will run about £900: £400 for materials, £400 for my crew and £100 profit for me.'

The Bristol contractor also does some measuring and figuring, and then says, 'I can do this job for £700: £300 for materials, £300 for my crew and £100 profit for me.'

The Liverpool contractor doesn't measure or figure but leans over to the Government official and whispers, "£2,700."

The official, incredulous, says, 'You didn't even measure like the other guys! How did you come up with such a high figure?'

The Liverpool contractor whispers back, '£1000 for me, £1000 for you, and we hire the guy from Bristol to fix the wall.'

'Done!' replies the government official.
And that, my friends, ... is how it all works.

In A Dublin Bar

A large woman, wearing a sleeveless sundress, walked into a bar in Dublin. She raised her right arm, revealing a huge, hairy armpit as she pointed to all the people sitting at the bar and asked,
"What man here will buy a woman drink?"
The bar went silent as the patrons tried to ignore her. But down at the end of the bar, an owly-eyed drunk slammed his hand down on the counter and bellowed,
"Give the ballerina a drink!"
The bartender poured the drink, and the woman chugged it down.
She turned to the patrons and again pointed around at all of them,
Revealing the same hairy armpit, and asked,
"What man here will buy a lady a drink?"
Once again, the same little drunk slapped his money down on the bar and said, "Give the ballerina another drink!"
The bartender approached the little drunk and said, "Tell me, Paddy, it's your business if you want to buy the lady a drink, but why do you keep calling her the ballerina?"
The drunk replied,
"Sure enough, any woman who can lift her leg that high has got to be a ballerina!"

☺ @ ☺

A Well-planned Retirement

Outside England's Bristol Zoo there is a parking lot for 150 cars and 8 buses. For 25 years, its parking fees were managed by a very pleasant attendant. The fees were for cars £1.40, for buses £7.

Then, one day, after 25 solid years of never missing a day of work, he just didn't show up; so the Zoo Management called the City Council and asked it to send them another attendant.

The Council did some research and replied that the parking lot was the Zoo's own responsibility.

The Zoo advised the Council that the attendant was a City employee.

The City Council responded that the lot attendant had never been on the City payroll.

Meanwhile, sitting in his villa somewhere on the coast of Spain or France or Italy ... is a man who'd apparently had a ticket machine installed completely on his own and then had simply begun to show up every day, commencing to collect and keep the parking fees, estimated at about £560 per day -- for 25 years.

Assuming 7 days a week, this amounts to just over 7 million pounds ... and no one even knows his name.

☺ @ ☺

Pay up!

On Thursday, 24th January 2002 , Derek Guille broadcast this story on his afternoon program on ABC radio.

In March 1999 a man living in Kandos (near Mudgee in NSW, Australia) received a bill for his as yet unused gas line stating that he owed $0.00.

He ignored it and threw it away. In April he received another bill and threw that one away too.

The following month the gas company sent him a very nasty note stating that they were going to cancel his gas line if he didn't send them $0.00 by return mail.

He called them, talked to them, and they said it was a computer error and they would take care of it.

The following month he decided that it was about time that he tried out the troublesome gas line figuring that if there was usage on the account it would put an end to this ridiculous predicament.

However, when he went to use the gas, it had been cut off.

He called the gas company who apologised for the computer error once again and said that they would take care of it. The next day he got a bill for $0.00 stating that payment was now overdue.

Assuming that having spoken to them the previous day the latest bill was yet another mistake, he ignored it, trusting that the company would be as good as their word and sort the problem out.

The next month he got a bill for $0.00. This bill also stated that he had 10 days to pay his account or the company would have to take steps to recover the debt.

Finally, giving in, he thought he would beat the gas company at their own game and mailed them a cheque for $0.00. The computer duly processed his account and returned a statement to the effect that he now owed the Gas company nothing at all.

A week later, the manager of the Mudgee branch of the Westpac Banking Corporation called our hapless friend and asked him what he was doing writing cheque for $0.00.

After a lengthy explanation the bank manager replied that the $0.00 cheque had caused their cheque processing software to fail. The bank could therefore not process ANY cheques they had received from ANY of their customers that day because the cheque for $0.00 had caused the computer to crash.

The following month the man received a letter from the gas company claiming that his cheque had bounced and that he now owed them $0.00 and unless he sent a cheque by return mail they would take immediate steps to recover the debt.

At this point, the man decided to file a debt harassment claim against the gas company. It took him nearly two hours to convince the clerks at the local courthouse that he was not joking.

They subsequently helped him in the drafting of statements which were considered substantive evidence of the aggravation and difficulties he had been forced to endure during this debacle.

The matter was heard in the Magistrate's Court in Mudgee and the outcome was this:

The gas company was ordered to:

[1] Immediately rectify their computerised accounts system or show cause, within 10 days, why the matter should not be referred to a higher Court for consideration under Company Law.

[2] Pay the bank dishonour fees incurred by the man.

[3] Pay the bank dishonour fees incurred by all the Westpac clients whose cheques had been bounced on the day our friend's had been processed.

[4] Pay the claimant's court costs; and

[5] Pay the claimant a total of $1500 per month for the 5 month period March to July inclusive as compensation for the aggravation they had caused their client to suffer.

And all this over $0.00.

☺ @ ☺

Where There's A Will . . .

A farmer stopped by the local garage to have his truck fixed. They couldn't do it while he waited, so he said he didn't live far and would just walk home.

On the way home he stopped at B & Q and bought a bucket and a gallon of paint. He then stopped by the market and picked up a couple of chickens and a goose. However, struggling outside the market he now had a problem - how to carry his entire purchases home.

While he was scratching his head he was approached by a little old lady who told him she was lost. She asked, 'Can you tell me how to get to Church Lane ?'

The farmer said, 'Well, as a matter of fact, my farm is very close to the lane I would walk you there but I can't carry this lot.'

The old lady suggested, 'Why don't you put the can of paint in the bucket. Carry the bucket in one hand, put a chicken under each arm and carry the goose in your other hand?'

'Why thank you very much,' he said and proceeded to walk the old girl home.

On the way he says 'Let's take my short cut and go down this alley. We'll be there in no time.'

The little old lady looked him over cautiously then said, 'I am a lonely widow without a husband to defend me... How do I know that when we get in the alley you won't hold me up against the wall, pull up my skirt, and have your way with me?'

The farmer said, 'Jeez, lady! I'm carrying a bucket, a gallon of paint, two chickens, and a goose. How in the world could I possibly hold you up against the wall and do that?'

The old lady replied, 'Set the goose down, cover him with the bucket, put the paint on top of the bucket, and I'll hold the chickens!!!'

☺ @ ☺

Tables Turned

A lawyer boarded an aeroplane in New Orleans with a box of frozen crabs and asked a blond stewardess to take care of them for him.

She took the box and promised to put it in the crew's refrigerator. He advised her that he was holding her personally responsible for them staying frozen, mentioning in a very haughty manner that he was a lawyer, and proceeded to rant at her about what would happen if she let them thaw out.

Needless to say, she was annoyed by his behaviour. Shortly before landing in New York, she used the intercom to announce to the entire cabin:

"Would the lawyer who gave me the crabs, in New Orleans, please raise your hand.

Not one hand went up .... so she took them home and ate them.

Two lessons here:

1. Lawyers aren't as smart as they think they are.

2. Blonds aren't as dumb as most folk think.

☺ @ ☺

The Evening news is where they begin with 'Good evening', and then proceed to tell you why it isn't.

A Punjabi lawyer working in the UK wrote to his wife in India...

Dear Sunita Darling,
I can't send you my salary this month because the global market crisis has affected my Company's performance, so I am sending 100 kisses.

You are my sweetheart,
please adjust.

Your loving husband,
JITA SINGH

His wife replied...

TINKU KE PAPPA ,

Thanks for the 100 kisses.
Below is the list of expenses I paid with the Kisses...:

1. The Milk man agreed on 2 kisses for one month's milk.

2. The electricity man agreed not to disconnect only after 7 kisses.

3. Your landlord Balkar Singh comes every day to take 2 or 3 kisses instead of the monthly rent.

4. Supermarket owner Jaswant Singh did not accept kisses only, so I gave him "other items", I hope you understand...

5. Miscellaneous expenses 40 kisses.

Please don't worry about me, I still have a balance of 35 kisses and I hope I can survive the month using this balance...
Shall I plan the same for the next month?!

Those Wonderful Church Bulletins

They're Back! Those wonderful Church Bulletins! Thank God for church ladies with typewriters. These sentences (with all the BLOOPERS) actually appeared in church bulletins or were announced in church services:

The Fasting & Prayer Conference includes meals.

The sermon this morning: 'Jesus Walks on the Water.' The sermon tonight: 'Searching for Jesus.'

Ladies, don't forget the rummage sale.. It's a chance to get rid of those things not worth keeping around the house. Bring your husbands.

Remember in prayer the many who are sick of our community. Smile at someone who is hard to love. Say 'Hell' to someone who doesn't care much about you.

Don't let worry kill you off - let the Church help.

Miss Charlene Mason sang 'I will not pass this way again,' giving obvious pleasure to the congregation.

For those of you who have children and don't know it, we have a nursery downstairs.

Next Thursday there will be tryouts for the choir. They need all the help they can get.

Irving Benson and Jessie Carter were married on October 24 in the church. So ends a friendship that began in their school days.

A bean supper will be held on Tuesday evening in the church hall. Music will follow.

At the evening service tonight, the sermon topic will be 'What Is Hell?' Come early and listen to our choir practice

---

Eight new choir robes are currently needed due to the addition of several new members and to the deterioration of some older ones.

Scouts are saving aluminium cans, bottles and other items to be recycled. Proceeds will be used to cripple children.

Please place your donation in the envelope along with the deceased person you want remembered.

The church will host an evening of fine dining, super entertainment and gracious hostility.

Potluck supper Sunday at 5:00 pm - prayer and medication to follow.

The ladies of the Church have cast off clothing of every kind. They may be seen in the basement on Friday afternoon.

This evening at 7 pm there will be a hymn singing in the park across from the Church. Bring a blanket and come prepared to sin.

Ladies Bible Study will be held Thursday morning at 10 am. All ladies are invited to lunch in the Fellowship Hall after the B. S. is done.

The pastor would appreciate it if the ladies of the Congregation would lend him their electric girdles for the pancake breakfast next Sunday.

Low Self Esteem Support Group will meet Thursday at 7 pm. Please use the back door.

The eighth-graders will be presenting Shakespeare's Hamlet in the Church basement Friday at 7 pm.. The congregation is invited to attend this tragedy.

Weight Watchers will meet at 7 pm at the First Presbyterian Church. Please use large double door at the side entrance.

The Associate Minister unveiled the church's new campaign slogan last Sunday:
"I Upped My Pledge - Up Yours".

☺ @ ☺

Boots lost a van load of Viagra a couple of weeks ago.   Nicked. Police are looking for a gang of hardened criminals.
Daily Telegraph (Your Money) - 25 September 2010

Critical Thinking At Its Best!

Woman: Do you drink beer?
Man: Yes.
Woman: How many beers a day?
Man: Usually about 3.
Woman: How much do you pay per beer?
Man: $5.00 which includes a tip.
Woman: And how long have you been drinking?
Man: About 20 years, I suppose.
Woman: So a beer costs $5 and you have 3 beers a day which puts your spending each month at $450. In one year, it would be approximately $5400. Correct?
Man: Correct.
Woman: If in 1 year you spend $5400, not accounting for inflation, the past 20 years puts your spending at $108,000, correct?
Man: Correct.
Woman: Do you know that if you didn't drink so much beer, that money could have been put in a step-up interest savings account and after accounting for compound interest for the past 20 years, you could have now bought a Ferrari?
Man: Do you drink beer?
Woman: No.
Man: Where's your Ferrari?

☺ @ ☺

What Good Friends Are For

A man brings his best buddy home for dinner unannounced at 5:30 after work. His wife screams at him as his friend listens in.

"My hair & makeup are not done, the house is a mess, the dishes are not done, I'm still in my pajamas and I can't be bothered with cooking tonight! What the hell did you bring him home for?"

"Because he's thinking of getting married."

Brochure circulated by a 5-Star Chinese Hotel

Getting There:

Our representative will make you wait at the airport. The bus to the hotel runs along the lake shore. Soon you will feel pleasure in passing water. You will know that you are getting near the hotel, because you will go round the bend. The manager will await you in the entrance hall. He always tries to have intercourse with all new guests.

The hotel:

This is a family hotel, so children are very welcome. We of course are always pleased to accept adultery. Highly skilled nurses are available in the evenings to put down your children. Guests are invited to conjugate in the bar and expose themselves to others. But please note that ladies are not allowed to have babies in the bar. We organize social games, so no guest is ever left alone to play with them self.

The Restaurant:

Our menus have been carefully chosen to be ordinary and unexciting. At dinner, our quartet will circulate from table to table, and fiddle with you.

Your Room:

Every room has excellent facilities for your private parts. In winter, every room is on heat. Each room has a balcony offering views of outstanding obscenity. You will not be disturbed by traffic noise, since the road between the hotel and the lake is used only by pederasts.

Bed

Your bed has been made in accordance with local tradition. If you have any other ideas please ring for the chambermaid. Please take advantage of her. She will be very pleased to squash your shirts, blouses and underwear. If asked, she will also squeeze your trousers.

Above all:

When you leave us at the end of your holiday, you will have no hope. You will struggle to forget it."

☺ @ ☺

Why I Mow My Own Lawn

One day, shortly after joining the PGA tour in 1965, Lee Trevino, a professional golfer and married man, was at his home in Dallas, Texas mowing his front lawn, as he always did. A lady driving by in a big, shiny Cadillac stopped in front of his house, lowered the window and asked, "Excuse me, do you speak English?"
Lee responded, "Yes Ma'am, I do."

The lady then asked, "What do you charge to do yard work?"
Lee said, "Well, the lady in this house lets me sleep with her."
The lady hurriedly put the car into gear and sped off.

☺ @ ☺

Sensually Subtle

Have you ever seen a twenty pound note all crumpled up?" asked the wife.
"No," I said.
She gave me a sexy little smile, slowly reached into her cleavage and pulled out a crumpled twenty pound note.
"Have you ever seen a fifty pound note all crumpled up?" she asked.
"No," I said.
She gave me another sexy little smile, seductively reached into her knickers and pulled out a crumpled fifty pound note.

"Now," she said, "have you ever seen 30,000 pounds all crumpled up?"
"No," I said, intrigued.

"Well, go and take a quick look in the garage."

☺ @ ☺

How to Write Good

Avoid alliteration. Always.
Prepositions are not words to end sentences with.
Avoid clichés like the plague. (They're old hat.)
Employ the vernacular.
Eschew ampersands & abbreviations, etc.
Parenthetical remarks (however relevant) are unnecessary.
It is wrong to ever split an infinitive.
Contractions aren't necessary.
Foreign words and phrases are not apropos.
One should never generalize.
Eliminate quotations. As Ralph Waldo Emerson once said: "I hate quotations. Tell me what you know."
Comparisons are as bad as clichés.
Don't be redundant; don't use more words than necessary; it's highly superfluous.
Profanity sucks.
Be more or less specific.
Understatement is always best.
Exaggeration is a billion times worse than understatement.
One-word sentences? Eliminate.
Analogies in writing are like feathers on a snake.
The passive voice is to be avoided.
Go around the barn at high noon to avoid colloquialisms.
Even if a mixed metaphor sings, it should be derailed.
Who needs rhetorical questions?

☺ @ ☺

Bunk-Up

Sir: Tom Hollander's story ('Strangers on a train', 13 October) reminded me of a true story from a while ago. An ex-officer in the Life Guards was travelling on a night sleeper train in the US. He was allocated a top bunk and as he climbed into it to retire he saw that there was an attractive woman in the bunk below.

He tossed and turned for a while before plucking up courage to lean over to pull back her curtain a couple of inches. He said: 'Madam, I am a man of few words — do you or don't you?' She looked up at him with some surprise and replied, 'Not usually, but you've talked me into it...'

Letter to The Times

☺ @ ☺

British Newspapers

The Times --- is read by the people who run the country.

The Daily Mirror --- is read by the people who think they run the country.

The Guardian --- is read by the people who think they ought to run the country.

The Morning Star --- is read by the people who think the country ought to be run by another country.

The Independent --- is read by people who don't know who runs the country but are sure they're doing it wrong.

The Daily Mail --- is read by the wives of the people who run the country.

The Financial Times --- is read by the people who own the country.

The Daily Express --- is read by the people who think the country ought to be run as it used to be run.

The Daily Telegraph --- is read by the people who still think it is their country.

The Sun's readers --- don't care who runs the country providing she has big boobs.

Things Getting you Down?

Well Then, Consider These . .READ ON!!

In a hospital's Intensive Care Unit, patients always died in the same bed, on Sunday morning, at about 11:00 am, regardless of their medical condition. This puzzled the doctors and some even thought it had something to do with the supernatural. No one could solve the mystery as to why the deaths occurred around 11:00 am Sunday, so a worldwide team of experts was assembled to investigate the cause of the incidents The next Sunday morning, a few minutes before 11:00 am all of the doctors and nurses nervously waited outside the ward to see for themselves what the terrible phenomenon was all about. Some were holding wooden crosses, prayer books, and other holy objects to ward off the evil spirits Just when the clock struck 11:00, Fernando Rodriguez , the part-time Sunday sweeper, entered the ward and unplugged the life support system so he could use the vacuum cleaner.

Still Having a Bad Day?

The average cost of rehabilitating a seal after the Exxon Valdez Oil spill in Alaska was $80,000.00 At a special ceremony, two of the most expensively saved animals were being released back into the wild amid cheers and applause from onlookers.. A minute later, in full view, a killer whale ate them both.

Still think you are having a Bad Day?

A woman came home to find her husband in the kitchen shaking frantically, almost in a dancing frenzy, with some kind of wire running from his waist towards the electric kettle. Intending to jolt him away from the deadly current, she ran outside and grabbed a handy plank of wood and smacked him with it, breaking his arm in two places. Up to that moment, he had been happily listening to his iPod

Are You OK Now? - No?

Two animal rights defenders were protesting the cruelty of sending pigs to a slaughterhouse in Bonn, Germany. Suddenly, all two thousand pigs broke loose and escaped through a broken fence, stampeding madly. The two helpless protesters were trampled to death.

What? STILL having a Bad Day?

Iraqi terrorist Khay Rahnajet didn't pay enough postage on a letter bomb. It came back with 'Return to Sender' stamped on it. Forgetting it was the bomb; he opened it and was blown to bits.

There, Now You're Feeling Better?

☺ @ ☺

The Wellie Boots

Did you hear about the Pre-School teacher who after a particularly frustrating day in the classroom was helping one of the children put on his "Wellie boots"?

He asked for help and she could see why..

Even with her pulling and him pushing, the little Wellies still didn't want to go on.

By the time they got the second Wellie on, she had worked up a sweat. She almost cried when the little boy said, "Miss, they're on the wrong feet.

She looked, and sure enough, they were.

It wasn't any easier pulling the Wellies off than it was putting them on.

She managed to keep her cool as together they worked to get the Wellies back on, this time on the right feet..

He then announced, "These aren't my Wellies."

She bit her tongue rather than get right in his face and scream, 'Why didn't you say so?' like she wanted to.

Once again, she struggled to help him pull the ill-fitting Wellies off his little feet.

No sooner had they gotten the "Wellie's" off when he said, "They're my brother's Wellies, my mum made me wear 'them.'

Now she didn't know if she should laugh or cry.

But, she mustered up what grace and courage she had left to wrestle the Wellies on his feet yet again.

Helping him into his coat, she asked, "Now, where are your gloves?"

He said, "I stuffed 'them in the toes of my Wellies."

She will be eligible for parole in three years.

☺   @   ☺

Smart Policeman

A police motorcycle cop stops a driver for running a red light. The driver is a real jerk, steps out of his car and comes striding toward the officer, demanding to know why he is being harassed by the Gestapo!

So the officer calmly tells him of the red light violation. The motorist instantly goes on a tirade, questioning the officer's ancestry, sexual orientation, etc., in rather explicit offensive terms.

The tirade goes on without the officer saying anything. When the officer finishes writing the ticket he puts an "AH" in the lower right corner of the narrative portion of the ticket. He then hands it to the 'violator' for his signature. The guy signs the ticket angrily, and when presented with his copy points to the "AH" and demands to know what it stands for. The officer says, "That's so when we go to court, I'll remember that you're an asshole!"

Two months later they're in court. The 'violator' has a bad driving record and he is in danger of losing his license, so he hired a lawyer to represent him. On the stand the officer testifies to seeing the man run the red light. Under cross examination the defence attorney asks; "Officer is this a reasonable facsimile of the ticket that you issued to my client?"

Officer responds, "Yes, sir, that is the defendant's copy, his signature and mine, same number at the top."

Lawyer: "Officer, is there any particular marking or quotation on this ticket you don't normally make?"

"Yes, sir, in the lower right corner of the narrative there is an "AH," underlined."

"What does the "AH" stand for, officer?"

"Aggressive and hostile, Sir."

"Aggressive and hostile?"

"Yes, Sir."

"Officer, are you sure it doesn't stand for asshole?"

Well, sir, you know your client better than I do."

How often can one get an attorney to convict his own client?

Shortest College Essay

A college class was told they had to write a short story in as few words as possible. The short story had to cover the following three subjects:

        (1) Religion
        (2) Sexuality
        (3) Mystery

Below is the only story awarded an A+

"Good God! I'm pregnant. I wonder who did it?"

☺ @ ☺

Boom-Boom!

Apparently it's no longer politically correct to direct a joke at any racial or ethnic minority or nationality so try this one:

An Englishman, a Scotsman, an Irishman, a Welshman, a Latvian, a Turk, an Aussie, a German, a Yank, an Egyptian, a Japanese, a Mexican, a Spaniard, a Russian, a Pole, a Lithuanian, a Swede, a Finn, an Israeli, a Romanian, a Bulgarian, a Serb, a Swiss, a Greek, a Singaporean, an Italian, a Norwegian and an African went to a night club.

The bouncer said: "Sorry, I can't let you in without a Thai"

☺ @ ☺

Senior Road Trip

While on a road trip, an elderly couple stopped at a roadside restaurant for lunch. After finishing their meal, they left the restaurant, and resumed their trip.

When leaving, the elderly woman unknowingly left her glasses on the table, and she didn't miss them until they had been driving for about forty minutes.

By then, to add to the aggravation, they had to travel quite a distance before they could find a place to turn around, in order to return to the restaurant to retrieve her glasses.

All the way back, the elderly husband became the classic grouchy man. He fussed and complained, and scolded his wife relentlessly during the entire return drive.

The more he chided her, the more agitated he became. He just wouldn't let up for a single minute.

To her relief, they finally arrived at the restaurant. As the woman got out of the car, and hurried inside to retrieve her glasses, the old geezer yelled to her, "While you're in there, you might as well get my hat and the credit card."

☺   @   ☺

Upgrades

Dear Tech Support,

Last year I upgraded from Boyfriend to Husband and noticed a distinct slowdown in overall system performance, particularly in the flower and jewellery applications, which operated flawlessly under Boyfriend.

In addition, Husband uninstalled many other valuable programmes, such as Romance and Personal Attention and then installed undesirable programs such as Rugby, Football, Sailing and Continuous TV. Conversation no longer runs, and Housecleaning simply crashes the system. I've tried running Nagging to fix these problems, but to no avail.

What can I do?

Signed, Desperate

....

Dear Desperate,

First keep in mind, Boyfriend is an Entertainment Package, while Husband is an Operating System. Please enter the command: 'http: I Thought You Loved Me.html' and try to download Tears. Don't forget to install the Guilt update. If that application works as designed, Husband should then automatically run the applications Jewellery and Flowers, but remember - overuse of the above application can cause Husband to default to Grumpy Silence, Garden Shed or Beer. Beer is a very bad program that will download the Snoring Loudly Beta.

Whatever you do, DO NOT install Mother-in-law (it runs a virus in the background that will eventually seize control of all your system resources). Also, do not attempt to reinstall the Boyfriend program. These are unsupported applications and will crash Husband.

In summary, Husband is a great system, but it does have limited memory and cannot learn new applications quickly. It also tends to work better running one task at a time. You might consider buying additional software to improve memory and performance. We recommend Food and Hot Lingerie.

Good Luck,
Tech Support

☺   @   ☺

Notes to The Milkman

I've just had a baby, please leave another one.

Please leave an extra pint of paralysed milk.

Cancel one pint after the day after today.

Please don't leave any more milk. All they do is drink it.

Milkman, please close the gate behind you because the birds keep pecking the tops off the milk.

Milkman, please could I have a loaf but not bread today.

Please cancel milk. I have nothing coming into the house but two sons on the dole.

Sorry not to have paid your bill before, but my wife had a baby and I've been carrying it around in my pocket for weeks.

Sorry about yesterday's note. I didn't mean one egg and a dozen pints, but the other way round.

When you leave my milk please knock on my bedroom window and wake me because I want you to give me a hand to turn the mattress.

Please knock. My TV's broken down and I missed last night's Coronation Street. If you saw it, will you tell me what happened over a cup of tea?

My daughter says she wants a milkshake. Do you do it before you deliver or do I have to shake the bottle?

Please send me a form for cheap milk, for I have a baby two months old and did not know about it until a neighbour told me.

Please send me details about cheap milk as I am stagnant.

Milk is needed for the baby. Father is unable to supply it.

From now on please leave two pints every other day and one pint on the days in between, except Wednesdays and Saturdays when I don't want any milk.

My back door is open. Please put milk in 'fridge, get money out of cup in drawer and leave change on kitchen table in pence, because we want to play bingo tonight.

Please leave no milk today. When I say today, I mean tomorrow, for I wrote this note yesterday.

When you leave the milk please put the coal on the boiler, let dog out and put newspaper inside the screen door. P.S. Don't leave any milk.

No milk. Please do not leave milk at No. 14 either as he is dead until further notice.

☺ @ ☺

Cowboy Boots

An elderly couple, Margaret and Bert, moved to Texas . Bert always wanted a pair of authentic cowboy boots, so, seeing some on sale, he bought them and wore them home.

Walking proudly, he sauntered into the kitchen and said to his wife, "Notice anything different about me?"

Margaret looked him over. "Nope."

Frustrated, Bert stormed off into the bathroom, undressed and walked back into the kitchen completely naked except for the boots.

Again he asked Margaret, a little louder this time, "Notice anything different NOW?"

Margaret looked up and said in her best deadpan, "Bert, what's different? It's hanging down today, it was hanging down yesterday, it'll be hanging down again tomorrow."

Furious, Bert yelled, "AND DO YOU KNOW WHY IT'S HANGING DOWN, MARGARET?"

"Nope. Not a clue", she replied.

"IT'S HANGING DOWN, BECAUSE IT'S LOOKING AT MY NEW BOOTS!!!!"

Without missing a beat Margaret replied, "Shoulda bought a hat, Bert. Shoulda bought a hat."

☺ @ ☺

Customer Relations

The following is an actual exchange (reputedly!) of correspondence between a customer and the Irish Railway Company.

Gentlemen,
I have been riding your trains daily for the last two years, and the service on your line seems to be getting worse every day.

I am tired of standing in the aisle all the time on a 14-mile trip. I think the transportation system is worse than that enjoyed by people 2,000 years ago.

Yours truly,

Patrick Finnegan

Dear Mr. Finnegan,

We received your letter with reference to the shortcomings of our service and believe you are somewhat confused in your history.

The only mode of transportation 2,000 years ago was by foot.

Sincerely,

Irish Railway Company

Gentlemen,

I am in receipt of your letter, and I think you are the ones who are confused in your history. If you will refer to the Bible and the Book of David, 9th Chapter, you will find that Balaam rode to town on his ass.

That.... gentlemen, is something I have not been able to do on your train in the last two years!

Yours truly,

Patrick Finnegan.

☺ @ ☺

Best Comeback Response of the Year

If you ever testify in court, you might wish you could have been as sharp as this policeman.

He was being cross-examined by a defense attorney during a felony trial.

The lawyer was trying to undermine the police officer's credibility .....

Q: 'Officer --- did you see my client fleeing the scene?'

A: 'No sir. But I subsequently observed a person matching the description of the offender, running several blocks away.'

Q: 'Officer -- who provided this description?'

A: 'The officer who responded to the scene.'

Q: 'A fellow officer provided the description of this so-called offender. Do you trust your fellow officers?'

A: 'Yes, sir. With my life.'

Q: 'With your life? Let me ask you this then officer. Do you have a room where you change your clothes in preparation for your daily duties?'

A: 'Yes sir, we do!'

Q: 'And do you have a locker in the room?'

A: 'Yes sir, I do.'

Q: 'And do you have a lock on your locker?'

A: 'Yes sir.'

Q: 'Now why is it, officer, if you trust your fellow officers with your life, you find it necessary to lock your locker in a room you share with these same officers?'

A: 'You see, sir -- we share the building with the court complex, and sometimes lawyers have been known to walk through that room.'

The courtroom EXPLODED with laughter, and a prompt recess was called.

Winter Prediction

It's late fall and the Indians on a remote reservation in British Columbia asked their new chief if the coming winter was going to be cold or mild.

Since he was a chief in a modern society, he had never been taught the old secrets. When he looked at the sky, he couldn't tell what the winter was going to be like.

Nevertheless, to be on the safe side, he told his tribal community that the winter was indeed going to be cold and that the members of the village should collect firewood to be prepared.

But, being a practical leader, after several days, he got an idea. He went to the phone booth, called the Environment Canada National Weather Service and asked, 'Is the coming winter going to be cold?'

'It looks like this winter is going to be quite cold,' the meteorologist at the weather service responded.

So the chief went back to his people and told them to collect even more firewood in order to be prepared.

A week later, he called Environment Canada 's National Weather Service again.

'Does it still look like it is going to be a very cold winter?'

'Yes,' the man at National Weather Service again replied, 'it's going to be a very cold winter.'

The chief again went back to his people and ordered them to collect every scrap of firewood they could find.

Two weeks later, the chief called Environment Canada's National Weather Service again. 'Are you absolutely sure that the winter is going to be very cold?'

'Absolutely,' the man replied. 'It's looking more and more like it is going to be one of the coldest winters we've ever seen.'

'How can you be so sure?' the chief asked.

The weatherman replied, 'The Indians are collecting firewood like crazy.'

Remember this whenever you get advice from a government official!

☺   @   ☺

Woman Marine Pilot

The teacher gave her fifth grade class an assignment: Get their parents to tell them a story with a moral at the end of it. The next day, the kids came back and, one by one, began to tell their stories.

There were all the regular types of stuff: spilled milk and pennies saved. But then the teacher realized, much to her dismay, that only Janie was left.

"Janie, do you have a story to share?"

'Yes ma'am. My daddy told me a story about my Mummy. She was a Marine pilot in Desert Storm, and her plane got hit. She had to bail out over enemy territory, and all she had was a flask of whiskey, a pistol, and a survival knife.

She saluted her plane and drank the whiskey on the way down while watching her plane crash in the distance, and then her parachute landed her right in the middle of 20 Iraqi troops.

She shot 15 of them with the pistol, until she ran out of bullets, killed four more with the knife, till the blade broke, and then she killed the last Iraqi with her bare hands."

"Good Heavens,' said the horrified teacher. What did your Daddy tell you was the moral to this horrible story?"

"Don't mess with Mummy when she's been drinking."

☺ @ ☺

Brian Sullivan

A man walked out to the street and caught a taxi just going by. He got into the taxi, and the cabbie said, "Perfect timing. You're just like "Brian!

Passenger: "Who?"

Cabbie: "Brian Sullivan. He's a guy who did everything right all the time. Like my coming along when you needed a cab, things happen like that to Brian Sullivan, every single time."

Passenger: "There are always a few clouds over everybody."

Cabbie: "Not Brian Sullivan. He was a terrific athlete. He could have won the Grand Slam at tennis. He could golf with the pros. He sang like an opera baritone and danced like a Broadway star and you should have heard him play the piano. He was an amazing guy."

Passenger: "Sounds like he was something really special."

Cabbie: "There's more. He had a memory like a computer. He remembered everybody's birthday. He knew all about wine, which foods to order and which fork to eat them with. He could fix anything. Not like me. I change a fuse, and the whole street blacks out. But Brian Sullivan, he could do everything right."

Passenger: "Wow. Some guy then."

Cabbie: "He always knew the quickest way to go in traffic and avoid traffic jams. Not like me, I always seem to get stuck in them. But Brian, he never made a mistake, and he really knew how to treat a woman and make her feel good. He would never answer her back even if she was in the wrong; and his clothing was always immaculate, shoes highly polished too. He was the perfect man! He never made a mistake. No one could ever measure up to Brian Sullivan."

Passenger: "An amazing fellow. How did you meet him?"

Cabbie: "Well, I never actually met Brian. He died. I'm married to his widow."

Bath Night

A couple take in an 18-year-old girl as a lodger.

When she arrived, she asked if she could have a bath but the woman of the house told her they didn't have a bathroom, and that they usually fill a tin bath in front of the fire.

She then explained: "Monday night would be the best night to take a bath, as that's when my husband goes out to darts ,"

So the girl agreed to have her bath the following Monday.

Monday came, and sure enough her husband went to the pub for his darts match, the woman filled the tin bath and watched as the girl got undressed.

She was most surprised to see that the lass didn't have any pubic hair.

When her husband got home she told him about it.

He of course didn't believe her, so she said; "Look, next week I'll leave a gap in the curtains then you can see for yourself."

The following Monday filled the bath, while the girl got undressed, curiously the wife asked; "Do you shave...?"

"...No," replied the girl. "I've just never grown any hair down there. Do you have hair?"

"Oh, yes," said the woman, and she showed her, hers.

When the girl went to bed, the husband came in and the wife asked; "Well, did you see it?"

"Yes," he said, "but why the hell did you have to show her yours."

"Why not?" she said. "You've seen it all before."

"I know," he said, "but the whole darn darts team hadn't...!!"

☺ @ ☺

The Love Dress

A woman stopped by, unannounced, at her son's house.

She knocked on the door and then immediately walked in.. She was shocked to see her daughter-in-law lying on the couch, totally naked. Soft music was playing, and the aroma of perfume filled the room.

"What are you doing?!" she asked.
"I'm waiting for Mike to come home from work," the daughter-in-law answered.
"But you're naked!" the mother-in-law exclaimed.
"This is my love dress," the daughter-in-law explained.
"Love dress? But you're naked!"

"Mike loves me and wants me to wear this dress," she explained. "It excites him to no end. Every time he sees me in this dress, he instantly becomes romantic and ravages me for hours on end. He can't get enough of me"

The mother-in-law left.
When she got home, she undressed, showered, put on her best perfume, dimmed the lights, put on a romantic CD, and laid on the couch, waiting for her husband to arrive.
Finally, her husband came home. He walked in and saw her laying there so provocatively.

"What are you doing?" he asked.

"This is my love dress." she whispered sensually.

"Needs ironing," he said. "What's for dinner?"

He never heard the gun shot.

☺ @ ☺

A Brunette Joke

A brunette goes into a doctor's office and says, "Doctor, I don't know what's wrong with me." The doctor says, "Well, tell me your symptoms."

"Well, everything hurts. When I touch my nose it hurts (touching nose), when I touch my leg it hurts (touching leg), when I touch my arm it hurts (touching arm), it just hurts everywhere!" she said.

The doctor, after looking at her for a second, said, "Did you used to be a blonde?" The brunette said, "Why yes!"

The doctor said, "Your finger's broken."

Alcohol Abuse

A man is stopped by the police at midnight and asked where he's going.

"I'm on the way to listen to a lecture about the effects of alcohol and drug abuse on the human body."

The policeman asks, "Really? And who's going to give a lecture at this time of night?"

"My wife", comes the reply.

☺ @ ☺

English from Around The World

In a Bangkok temple:
IT IS FORBIDDEN TO ENTER A WOMAN, EVEN A FOREIGNER, IF DRESSED AS A MAN.

Cocktail lounge, Norway:
LADIES ARE REQUESTED NOT TO HAVE CHILDREN IN THE BAR.

Doctor's office, Rome:
SPECIALIST IN WOMEN AND OTHER DISEASES.

Dry cleaners, Bangkok:
DROP YOUR TROUSERS HERE FOR THE BEST RESULTS.

In a Nairobi restaurant:
CUSTOMERS WHO FIND OUR WAITRESSES RUDE OUGHT TO SEE THE MANAGER.

On the main road to Mombasa, leaving Nairobi:
TAKE NOTICE: WHEN THIS SIGN IS UNDER WATER, THIS ROAD IS IMPASSABLE.

On a poster at Kencom:
ARE YOU AN ADULT THAT CANNOT READ? IF SO WE CAN HELP.

In a City restaurant:
OPEN SEVEN DAYS A WEEK AND WEEKENDS.

In a cemetery:
PERSONS ARE PROHIBITED FROM PICKING FLOWERS FROM ANY BUT THEIR OWN GRAVES .

Tokyo hotel's rules and regulations:
GUESTS ARE REQUESTED NOT TO SMOKE OR DO OTHER DISGUSTING BEHAVIOURS IN BED.

On the menu of a Swiss restaurant:
OUR WINES LEAVE YOU NOTHING TO HOPE FOR.

In a Tokyo bar:
SPECIAL COCKTAILS - FOR THE LADIES WITH NUTS.

Hotel, Yugoslavia:
THE FLATTENING OF UNDERWEAR WITH PLEASURE IS THE JOB OF THE CHAMBERMAID.

Hotel, Japan:
YOU ARE INVITED TO TAKE ADVANTAGE OF THE CHAMBERMAID.

In the lobby of a Moscow hotel across from a Russian Orthodox monastery:
YOU ARE WELCOME TO VISIT THE CEMETERY WHERE FAMOUS RUSSIAN AND SOVIET COMPOSERS, ARTISTS AND WRITERS ARE BURIED DAILY EXCEPT THURSDAY.

Advertisement for donkey rides, Thailand:
WOULD YOU LIKE TO RIDE ON YOUR OWN ASS?

A sign posted in Germany's Black Forest:
IT IS STRICTLY FORBIDDEN ON OUR BLACK FOREST CAMPING SITE THAT PEOPLE OF DIFFERENT SEX, FOR INSTANCE, MEN AND WOMEN, LIVE TOGETHER IN ONE TENT UNLESS THEY ARE MARRIED WITH EACH OTHER FOR THIS PURPOSE.

Hotel, Zurich:
BECAUSE OF THE IMPROPRIETY OF ENTERTAINING GUESTS OF THE OPPOSITE SEX IN THE BEDROOM, IT IS SUGGESTED THAT THE LOBBY BE USED FOR THIS PURPOSE..

Airline ticket office, Copenhagen:
WE TAKE YOUR BAGS AND SEND THEM IN ALL DIRECTIONS.

A laundry in Rome:
LADIES, LEAVE YOUR CLOTHES HERE AND SPEND THE AFTERNOON HAVING A GOOD TIME.

☺ @ ☺

Repent, O Scottish Sinner

There was a Scottish painter named Smokey Macgregor who was very interested in making a penny where he could, so he often thinned down his paint to make it go a wee bit further.

As it happened, he got away with this for some time, but eventually the Baptist Church decided to do a big restoration job on the outside of one of their biggest buildings.

Smokey put in a bid, and, because his price was so low, he got the job. So he set about erecting the scaffolding and setting up the planks, and buying the paint and, yes, I am sorry to say, thinning it down with water...

Well, Smokey was up on the scaffolding, painting away, the job nearly completed, when suddenly there was a horrendous clap of thunder, the sky opened, and the rain poured down washing the thinned paint from all over the church and knocking Smokey clear off the scaffold to land on the lawn among the gravestones, surrounded by telltale puddles of the thinned and useless paint.

Smokey was no fool. He knew this was a judgment from the Almighty, so he got down on his knees and cried:

"Oh, Lord, forgive me; what should I do?"

And from the thunder, a mighty voice spoke..

"Repaint! Repaint! And thin no more!"

☺ @ ☺

When Insults Had Class

These glorious insults are from an era before the English language got boiled down to 4-letter words.

The exchange between Churchill & Lady Astor:

She said, "If you were my husband I'd give you poison."

He said, "If you were my wife, I'd drink it."

A member of Parliament to Disraeli: "Sir, you will either die on the gallows or of some unspeakable disease."

"That depends, Sir," said Disraeli, "whether I embrace your policies or your mistress."

"He had delusions of adequacy." *Walter Kerr*

"He has all the virtues I dislike and none of the vices I admire."
Winston Churchill

"I have never killed a man, but I have read many obituaries with great pleasure." *Clarence Darrow*

"He has never been known to use a word that might send a reader to the dictionary." - *William Faulkner (about Ernest Hemingway).*

"Thank you for sending me a copy of your book; I'll waste no time reading it." *Moses Hadas*

"I didn't attend the funeral, but I sent a nice letter saying I approved of it." *Mark Twain*

"He has no enemies, but is intensely disliked by his friends.." - *Oscar Wilde*

"I am enclosing two tickets to the first night of my new play; bring a friend.... if you have one." - George Bernard Shaw to Winston Churchill

"Cannot possibly attend first night, will attend second.... if there is one." - Winston Churchill, in response.

"I feel so miserable without you; it's almost like having you here." - *Stephen Bishop*

"He is a self-made man and worships his creator." *John Bright*

"I've just learned about his illness. Let's hope it's nothing trivial." *Irvin S. Cobb*

"He is not only dull himself; he is the cause of dullness in others." *Samuel Johnson*

"He is simply a shiver looking for a spine to run up."
Paul Keating

"In order to avoid being called a flirt, she always yielded easily."
Charles, Count Talleyrand

"He loves nature in spite of what it did to him." *Forrest Tucker*

"Why do you sit there looking like an envelope without any address on it?" *Mark Twain*

"His mother should have thrown him away and kept the stork."
Mae West

"Some cause happiness wherever they go; others, whenever they go.." *Oscar Wilde*

"He uses statistics as a drunken man uses lamp-posts... for support rather than illumination." *Andrew Lang*

"He has Van Gogh's ear for music." *Billy Wilder*

☺ @ ☺

Go to the Bottom of the Class

The following questions were set in last year's GED examination. These are genuine answers (from 16 year olds)

Q. Name the four seasons
A. Salt, pepper, mustard and vinegar

Q. Explain one of the processes by which water can be made safe to drink
A. Flirtation makes water safe to drink because it removes large pollutants like grit, sand, dead sheep and canoeists

Q. How is dew formed
A. The sun shines down on the leaves and makes them perspire

Q. What causes the tides in the oceans
A. The tides are a fight between the earth and the moon. All water tends to flow towards the moon, because there is no water on the moon, and nature abhors a vacuum. I forget where the sun joins the fight

Q. What guarantees may a mortgage company insist on
A. If you are buying a house they will insist that you are well endowed

Q. In a democratic society, how important are elections
A. Very important. Sex can only happen when a male gets an election

Q. What are steroids
A. Things for keeping carpets still on the stairs

Q. What happens to your body as you age
A. When you get old, so do your bowels and you get intercontinental

Q. What happens to a boy when he reaches puberty
A. He says goodbye to his boyhood and looks forward to his adultery

Q. Name a major disease associated with cigarettes
A. Premature death

Q. What is artificial insemination
A. When the farmer does it to the bull instead of the cow

Q. How can you delay milk turning sour
A. Keep it in the cow

Q. How are the main 20 parts of the body categorised (e.g. The abdomen)

A. The body is consisted into 3 parts - the brainium, the borax and the abdominal cavity. The brainium contains the brain, the borax contains the heart and lungs and the abdominal cavity contains the five bowels: A, E, I,O,U..

Q. What is the fibula?
A. A small lie

Q. What does 'varicose' mean?
A. Nearby

Q. What is the most common form of birth control?
A. Most people prevent contraception by wearing a condominium

Q. Give the meaning of the term 'Caesarean section'
A. The caesarean section is a district in Rome

Q. What is a seizure?
A. A Roman Emperor.

Q. What is a terminal illness?
A. When you are sick at the airport.

Q. Give an example of a fungus. What is a characteristic feature?
A. Mushrooms. They always grow in damp places and they look like umbrellas

Q. Use the word 'judicious' in a sentence to show you understand its meaning
A. Hands that judicious can be soft as your face.

Q. What does the word 'benign' mean?
A. Benign is what you will be after you be eight

☺ @ ☺

Incredible

In 1986, Peter Davies was on holiday in Kenya after graduating from Northwestern University ....

On a hike through the bush, he came across a young bull elephant standing with one leg raised in the air. The elephant seemed distressed, so Peter approached it very carefully. He got down on one knee, inspected the elephants foot, and found a large piece of wood deeply embedded in it. As carefully and as gently as he could, Peter worked the wood out with his knife, after which the elephant gingerly put down its foot.

The elephant turned to face the man, and with a rather curious look on its face, stared at him for several tense moments. Peter stood frozen, thinking of nothing else but being trampled.

Eventually the elephant trumpeted loudly, turned, and walked away.

Peter never forgot that elephant or the events of that day.

Twenty years later, Peter was walking through the Chicago Zoo with his teenage son. As they approached the elephant enclosure, one of the creatures turned and walked over to near where Peter and his son Cameron were standing.

The large bull elephant stared at Peter, lifted its front foot off the ground, then put it down. The elephant did that several times then trumpeted loudly, all the while staring at the man.

Remembering the encounter in 1986, Peter could not help wondering if this was the same elephant.

Peter summoned up his courage, climbed over the railing, and made his way into the enclosure.

He walked right up to the elephant and stared back in wonder.

The elephant trumpeted again, wrapped its trunk around one of Peter legs and slammed him against the railing, killing him instantly.

Probably wasn't the same elephant

☺ @ ☺

Hotdog

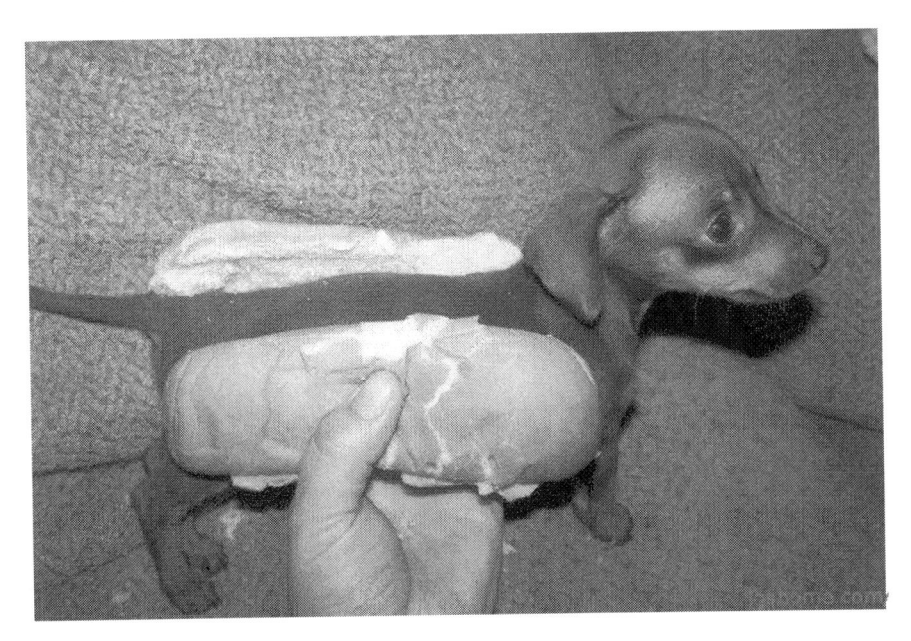

☺ @ ☺

Ponderisms

I used to eat a lot of natural foods until I learned that most people die of natural causes.

Gardening Rule: When weeding, the best way to make sure you are removing a weed and not a valuable plant is to pull on it. If it comes out of the ground easily, it is a valuable plant.

The easiest way to find something lost around the house is to buy a replacement.

Never take life seriously. Nobody gets out alive anyway.

There are two kinds of pedestrians: the quick and the dead.

Life is sexually transmitted.

The only difference between a rut and a grave is the depth.

Have you noticed since everyone has a camcorder these days no one talks about seeing UFOs like they used to?

Whenever I feel blue, I start breathing again

All of us could take a lesson from the weather. It pays no attention to criticism.

In the 60s, people took acid to make the world weird. Now the world is weird and people take Prozac to make it normal

How is it one careless match can start a forest fire, but it takes a whole box to start a campfire?

Who was the first person to look at a cow and say, "I think I'll squeeze these dangly things here, and drink whatever comes out?"

"Why is there a light in the fridge and not in the freezer?

If quizzes are quizzical, what are tests?

Do illiterate people get the full effect of Alphabet Soup?

Why doesn't glue stick to the inside of the bottle?

☺ @ ☺

History of Art in a Nutshell

☺ @ ☺

Enzo the Deaf Bookkeeper

Mafia Godfather finds out that his bookkeeper, Enzo, has cheated him out of 10 million bucks. His bookkeeper is deaf. That was the reason he got the job in the first place. It was assumed that Enzo would hear nothing that he might have to testify about in court.
When the Godfather goes to confront Enzo about his missing $10 million, he takes along his lawyer who knows sign language.

The Godfather tells the lawyer, "Ask him where the 10 million bucks is that he embezzled from me."
The lawyer, using sign language, asks Enzo where the money is.
Enzo signs back, "I don't know what you are talking about."
The lawyer tells the Godfather, "He says he doesn't know what you are talking about."
The Godfather pulls out a pistol, puts it to Enzo's temple and says, "Ask him again!"
The lawyer signs to Enzo, "He'll kill you if you don't tell him."
Enzo signs back, "OK. You win! The money is in a brown briefcase, buried behind the shed in my cousin Bruno's backyard in Calabria!"
The Godfather asks the lawyer, "What did he say?"
The lawyer replies, " He says you don't have the guts to pull the trigger."

☺ @ ☺

Chinese Proverb

Confucius say, "If you are in a book store and cannot find the book for which you search, you are obviously in the.....

☺ @ ☺

Explaining Taxes with Beer

It took a Professor in Economics.... maybe his students will now understand...hopefully.

Tax System explained in beer.

Suppose that every day, ten men go out for beer and the bill for all ten comes to $100. If they paid their bill the way we pay our taxes, it would go something like this

The first four men (the poorest) would pay nothing.
The fifth would pay $1.
The sixth would pay $3.
The seventh would pay $7.
The eighth would pay $12.
The ninth would pay $18.
The tenth man (the richest) would pay $59.

So, that's what they decided to do.

The ten men drank in the bar every day and seemed quite happy with the arrangement, until one day, the owner threw them a curve. 'Since you are all such good customers,' he said, 'I'm going to reduce the cost of your daily beer by $20. Drinks for the ten now cost just $80.

The group still wanted to pay their bill the way we pay our taxes

So the first four men were unaffected. They would still drink for free. But what about the other six men - the paying customers? How could they divide the $20 windfall so that everyone would get his 'fair share?'

They realized that $20 divided by six is $3.33. But if they subtracted that from everybody's share, then the fifth man and the sixth man would each end up being paid to drink his beer.

So, the bar owner suggested that it would be fair to reduce each man's bill by roughly the same amount, and he proceeded to work out the amounts each should pay. and so the fifth man, like the first four, now paid nothing (100% savings).
The sixth now paid $2 instead of $3 (33% savings).
The seventh now paid $ 5 instead of $7 (28%savings).
The eighth now paid $9 instead of $12 (25% savings).
The ninth now paid $14 instead of $18 (22% savings).
The tenth now paid $49 instead of $59 (16% savings).

Each of the six was better off than before. And the first four continued to drink for free. But once outside the restaurant, the men began to compare their savings.

'I only got a dollar out of the $ 20,'declared the sixth man. He pointed to the tenth man,' but he got $10!' 'Yeah, that's right,' exclaimed the fifth man. 'I only saved a dollar, too. It's unfair that he got ten times more than I!' 'That's true!!' shouted the seventh man. 'Why should he get $10 back when I got only two? The wealthy get all the breaks!' 'Wait a minute,' yelled the first four men in unison. 'We didn't get anything at all. The system exploits the poor!'

The nine men surrounded the tenth and beat him up.

The next night the tenth man didn't show up for drinks, so the nine sat down and had beers without him. But when it came time to pay the bill, they discovered something important. They didn't have enough money between all of them for even half of the bill!

And that, boys and girls, journalists and college professors, this is how our tax system works. The people who pay the highest taxes get the most benefit from a tax reduction. Tax them too much, attack them for being wealthy, and they just may not show up any more. In fact, they might start drinking overseas where the atmosphere is somewhat friendlier.

Indian School of Business

Rajpat (the father): Son, I want you to marry a girl of my choice.
Son: "I will choose my own bride!!!"
Rajpat: "But the girl is Bill Gates's daughter.."
Son: "Well, in that case... Ok"
Next Rajpat approaches Bill Gates.
Rajpat: "I have a husband for your daughter...."
Bill Gates: "But my daughter is too young to marry!!!!!"
Rajpat: "But this young man is a vice-president of the World Bank."
Bill Gates: "Ah, in that case... Ok"
Finally Rajpat goes to see the president of the World Bank.
Rajpat: "I have a young man to be recommended as a vice-president.."
President: "But I already have more vice- presidents than I need!"
Rajpat: "But this young man is Bill Gates's son-in-law."
President: "Ah, in that case... Ok"
And that my friend, is how Indians do business.

☺   @   ☺

Little Pig

This is a true story, indicating how fascinating the mind of a six year old is. They think so logically.

A teacher was reading the story of the Three Little Pigs to her class. She came to the part of the story where the first pig was trying to gather the building materials for his home. She read, "... and so the pig went up to the man with the wheelbarrow full of straw and said, 'Pardon me sir, but may I have some of that straw to build my house?'" The teacher paused......then asked the class, "And what do you think the man said?"

One little boy raised his hand and said very matter-of-factly "I think the man would have said, 'Well, blow me! A talking pig!'"

A Push

A man and his wife were awakened at 3:00 am by a loud pounding on the door. The man gets up and goes to the door where a drunken stranger, standing in the pouring rain, is asking for a push.

'Not a chance,' says the husband, 'it is 3:00 in the morning!' He slams the door and returns to bed.

'Who was that?' asked his wife.

'Just some drunk guy asking for a push,' he answers.

'Did you help him?' she asks.

'No, I did not, it is 3:00 in the morning and it is pouring rain out there!'

'Well, you have a short memory,' says his wife. 'Can't you remember about three months ago when we broke down, and those two guys helped us? I think you should help him, and you should be ashamed of yourself!'

The man does as he is told, gets dressed, and goes out into the pounding rain.

He calls out into the dark, 'Hello, are you still there?'

'Yes,' comes back the answer.

'Do you still need a push?' calls out the husband.

'Yes, please!' comes the reply from the dark.

'Where are you?' asks the husband.

'Over here on the swing,' replied the drunk.

Some of Murphy's Lesser-known Laws

1. Light travels faster than sound. This is why some people appear bright until you hear them speak.

2. Change is inevitable, except from a vending machine.

3. Those who live by the sword get shot by those who don't.

4. Nothing is foolproof to a sufficiently talented fool.

5. The 50-50-90 rule: Any time you have a 50-50 chance of getting something right, there's a 90% probability you'll get it wrong.

6. If you lined up all the cars in the world end to end, someone would be stupid enough to try to pass them, five or six at a time, on a hill, in the fog.

7. The things that come to those who wait will be the scraggly junk left by those who got there first.

8. The shin bone is a device for finding furniture in a dark room.

9. A fine is a tax for doing wrong. A tax is a fine for doing well.

10. When you go into court, you are putting yourself into the hands of 12 people who weren't smart enough to get out of jury duty.

☺   @   ☺

Who is your real friend?

This really works...! If you don't believe it, just try this experiment.
Put your dog and your wife in the boot of the car for an hour. When you finally open the boot, who is really happy to see you?

Farm Inspection

A rather cocky Department of Agriculture representative stopped at a farm and spoke with the old farmer.
He told the farmer, 'I need to inspect your farm.' The old farmer said,
'OK, but don't go in that field right over yonder.' The Agriculture representative said, 'Mister, I have the authority of the State Government with me. See this badge? This badge means I am allowed to go WHEREVER I WISH on any agricultural land. Have I made myself clear? Do you understand?'

The farmer nodded politely and went about his farm chores.

Half an hour later, the farmer heard loud screams and saw the Agriculture Rep running for the fence and close behind was the farmer's huge-horned prize bull. The bull was gaining on the Agriculture Rep with every step. The Rep was clearly terrified, so farmer immediately threw down his tools, ran to the fence and shouted out:

'Your badge! Your badge! Show him your badge!'

☺ @ ☺

Dead Duck

A woman brought a very limp duck into a veterinary surgeon. As she laid her pet on the table, the vet pulled out his stethoscope and listened to the bird's chest.

After a moment or two, the vet shook his head sadly and said, 'I'm so sorry, your duck, Cuddles, has passed away.' The distressed owner wailed, 'Are you sure'? 'Yes, I am sure. The duck is dead,' he replied.

'How can you be so sure'? she protested. 'I mean, you haven't done any testing on him or anything. He might just be in a coma or something.'

The vet rolled his eyes, turned around and left the room, and returned a few moments later with a black Labrador Retriever. As the duck's owner looked on in amazement, the dog stood on his hind legs, put his front paws on the examination table and sniffed the duck from top to bottom . He then looked at the vet with sad eyes and shook his head. The vet patted the dog and took it out, and returned a few moments later with a cat. The cat jumped up on the table and also sniffed delicately at the bird from head to foot. The cat sat back on it haunches, shook its head, meowed softly and strolled out of the room.

The vet looked at the woman and said, 'I'm sorry, but as I said, this is most definitely, 100 percent certifiably, a dead duck.' Then the vet turned to his computer terminal hit a few keys and produced a bill, which he handed to the woman. The duck's owner, still in shock, took the bill. '£150!' she cried. '£150 just to tell me my duck is dead'? 'The vet shrugged. I'm sorry. If you'd taken my word for it, the bill would have been £20, but with the lab report and the cat scan, it's now £150.'

☺ @ ☺

Why men don't talk to each other in public toilets.

The other day I needed to pay a visit, so I found a public toilet that had two cubicles. One of the doors was locked so I went into the other one, closed the door, dropped my trousers and sat down. A voice came from the cubicle next to me: 'Hello mate, how are you doing?'

Although I thought that it was a bit strange, I didn't want to be rude, so I replied 'Not too bad thanks.'

After a short pause, I heard the voice again 'So, what are you up to?'

Again I answered, somewhat reluctantly, 'Just having a quick poo. How about yourself?'

The next thing I heard him say was - 'Sorry mate, I'll have to call you back. I've got some idiot in the cubicle next to me answering everything I say."

☺ @ ☺

High Hotel Bill

Next time you think your hotel bill is too high you might want to consider this...

Husband and wife are travelling by car from Key West to Boston. After almost twenty-four hours on the road, They're too tired to continue, and they decide to stop for a rest. They stop at a nice hotel and take a room, but they only plan to sleep for four hours and then get back on the road.

When they check out four hours later, the desk clerk hands them a bill for $350.00.

The man explodes and demands to know why the charge is so high. He tells the clerk although it's a nice hotel, the rooms certainly aren't worth $350.00!

When the clerk tells him $350.00 is the standard rate, the man insists on speaking to the Manager. The Manager appears, listens to the man, and then explains that the hotel has an Olympic-sized pool and a huge conference centre that were available for the husband and wife to use.

'But we didn't use them,' the man complains.

'Well, they are here, and you could have,' explains the Manager. He goes on to explain they could have taken in one of the shows for which the hotel is famous.

'The best entertainers from New York, Hollywood and Las Vegas perform here,' the Manager says.

'But we didn't go to any of those shows,' complains the man again.

'Well, we have them, and you could have,' the Manager replies. No matter what amenity the Manager mentions, the man replies, 'But we didn't use it!'

The Manager is unmoved, and eventually the man gives up and agrees to pay. He writes a cheque and gives it to the Manager.

The Manager is surprised when he looks at the check. 'But sir,' he says, 'this check is only made out for $50.00.'

'That's correct,' says the man. 'I charged you $300.00 for sleeping with my wife.'

'But I didn't!' exclaims the Manager.

'Well, too bad,' the man replies. 'She was here and you could have.'

☺ @ ☺

Knickers

Little Emily went home from school and told her mum that the boys kept asking her to do cartwheels because she's very good at them.
Mum said, "You should say "No" -they only want to look at your knickers."
Emily said, "I know they do. That's why I hide them in my bag"!

Duck Joke

A duck walks into a pub and orders a pint of beer and a ham sandwich. the barman looks at him and says,

"Hang on! You're a duck."

"I see your eyes are working," replies the duck.

"And you can talk!" exclaims the barman.

"I see your ears are working, too," says the duck.

"Now if you don't mind, can I have my beer and my sandwich please?"

"Certainly, sorry about that," says the barman as he pulls the duck's pint.

"It's just we don't get many ducks in this pub... What are you doing round this way?"

"I'm working on the building site across the road," explains the duck.

"I'm a plasterer."

The flabbergasted barman cannot believe the duck and wants to learn more, but takes the hint when the duck pulls out a newspaper from his bag and proceeds to read it.

So, the duck reads his paper, drinks his beer, eats his sandwich, bids the barman good day and leaves.

The same thing happens for two weeks.

Then one day the circus comes to town.

The ringmaster comes into the pub for a pint and the barman says to him: "You're with the circus, aren't you? Well, I know this duck that could be just brilliant in your circus. He talks, drinks beer, eats sandwiches, reads the newspaper and everything!"

"Sounds marvellous," says the ringmaster, handing over his business card. "Get him to give me a call."

So the next day when the duck comes into the pub the barman says, "Hey Mr. Duck, I reckon I can line you up with a top job."

"I'm always looking for the next job," says the duck. "Where is it?"

"At the circus," says the barman.

"The circus?" repeats the duck.

"That's right,"

"The circus?" the duck asks again. "With the big tent?"

"Yeah," the barman replies.

"With all the animals who live in cages, and performers who live in caravans?" says the duck.

"Of course," the barman replies.

"And the tent has canvas sides and a big canvas roof with a hole in the middle?" persists the duck.

"That's right!" says the barman.

The duck shakes his head in amazement, and says .. . .

"Why in Heaven's name would they want a plasterer??!"

Heart-warming Lawyer Story

One afternoon a lawyer was riding in his limousine when he saw two men along the road-side eating grass. Disturbed, he ordered his driver to stop and he got out to investigate.

He asked one man, "Why are you eating grass?"

"We don't have any money for food," the poor man replied. "We have to eat grass."

"Well, then, you can come with me to my house and I'll feed you," the lawyer said.

"But sir, I have a wife and two children with me. They are over there, under that tree."

"Bring them along," the lawyer replied.

Turning to the other poor man he stated, "You come with us, also."

The second man, in a pitiful voice, then said, "But sir, I also have a wife and SIX children with me !"

"Bring them all, as well," the lawyer answered.

They all entered the car, which was no easy task, even for a car as large as the limousine was.

Once under way, one of the poor fellows turned to the lawyer and said, "Sir, you are too kind."

"Thank you for taking all of us with you.

The lawyer replied, "Glad to do it. "You'll really love my place.

"The grass is almost a foot high"

New Element Discovered

Cambridge University researchers have discovered the heaviest element yet known to science. The new element, Governmentium (symbol=Gv), has one neutron, 25 assistant neutrons, 88 deputy neutrons and 198 assistant deputy neutrons, giving it an atomic mass of 312.

These 312 particles are held together by forces called morons, which are surrounded by vast quantities of lepton-like particles called pillocks. Since Governmentium has no electrons, it is inert. However, it can be detected because it impedes every reaction with which it comes into contact.

A tiny amount of Governmentium can cause a reaction that would normally take less than a second, to take from 4 days to 4 years to complete.
Governmentium has a normal half-life of 2 to 6 years. It does not decay, but instead undergoes a reorganisation in which a portion of the assistant neutrons and deputy neutrons exchange places.

In fact, Governmentium's mass will actually increase over time, since each reorganisation will cause more morons to become neutrons, forming isodopes. This characteristic of moron promotion leads some scientists to believe that Governmentium is formed whenever morons reach a critical concentration. This hypothetical quantity is referred to as a critical morass. When catalysed with money, Governmentium becomes Administratium (symbol=Ad), an element that radiates just as much energy as Governmentium, since it has half as many pillocks but twice as many morons.

☺   @   @

Jonathan Ross has been accused of shoplifting a kitchen utensil from Tesco. Ross says it was a whisk he was prepared to take..

Friends For Dinner

A group of 40 year old buddies discuss and discuss where they should meet for dinner. Finally it is agreed upon that they should eat at the Gasthof zum Löwen restaurant because the waitresses there have low cut blouses and nice breasts.

10 years later, at 50 years of age, the group meets again and once again they discuss and discuss where they should have dinner. Finally it is agreed upon that they should eat at the Gasthof zum Löwen because the food there is very good and the wine selection is good also.

10 years later at 60 years of age, the group meets again and once again they discuss and discuss where they should meet for dinner. Finally it is agreed upon that they should go to the Gasthof zum Löwen because they can eat there in peace and quiet and the restaurant is smoke free.

10 years later, at 70 years of age, the group meets again and once again they discuss and discuss where they should have dinner. Finally it is agreed upon that they should eat at the Gasthof zum Löwen because the restaurant is wheel chair accessible and they even have an elevator.

10 years later, at 80 years of age, the group meets again and once again they discuss and discuss where they should meet for dinner. Finally it is agreed upon that it would be a great idea if they ate at the Gasthof zum Löwen because they have never been there before.

☺ @ ☺

A husband says to his wife, "what would you do if I won the Lottery?"
She says, "I'd take half, then leave you."
"Excellent," he replies,
"I won £12 , here's £6 - now clear off!"

Baby's First Doctor's Visit

A woman and a baby were in the doctor's examining room, waiting for the doctor to come in for the baby's first exam.

The doctor arrived, and examined the baby, checked his weight, and being a little concerned, asked if the baby was breast-fed or bottle-fed.

'Breast-fed,' she replied.

'Well, strip down to your waist,' the doctor ordered.

She did. He pinched her nipples, pressed, kneaded, and rubbed both breasts for a while in a very professional and detailed examination.

Motioning to her to get dressed, the doctor said,

'No wonder this baby is underweight. You don't have any milk.'

I know,' she said, 'I'm his Grandma, but I'm really glad I came.'

☺ @ ☺

Quick-witted

A man in the greengrocers' tries to buy half a cauliflower. The very young new assistant tells him that they sell only whole cauliflowers. The man persists and asks to see the manager. The boy says he'll ask his manager about it.

Walking into the back room, the boy said to his manager, 'Some idiot out there wants to buy half a cauliflower.'

As he finished his sentence, he turned to find the man standing right behind him, so he added, 'And this gentleman wants to buy the other half.'

The manager approved the deal, and the man went on his way.

Later the manager said to the boy, 'I was impressed with the way you got yourself out of that situation earlier. We like people who think on their feet here. Where are you from, son?'

'Cardiff, sir,' the boy replied.

'Well, why did you leave Cardiff?' the manager asked.

The boy said, 'Sir, there's nothing but whores and rugby players down there.'

'Really?' said the manager. 'My wife is from Cardiff.'

'You're kidding?' replied the boy. 'Who'd she play for?

☺ @ ☺

Yuletide Tradition

One particular Christmas season a long time ago, Santa was getting ready for his annual trip ... but there were problems everywhere. Four of his elves got sick, and the trainee elves did not produce the toys as fast as the regular ones so Santa was beginning to feel the pressure of being behind schedule.

Then Mrs. Claus told Santa that her mother was coming to visit. This stressed Santa even more.

When he went to harness the reindeer, he found that three of them were about to give birth and two had jumped the fence and were out, heaven knows where. More stress.

Then when he began to load the sleigh one of the boards cracked and the toy bag fell to the ground and scattered the toys.

So, frustrated, Santa went into the house for a cup of coffee and a shot of whiskey. When he went to the cupboard, he discovered that the elves had hidden the liquor and there was nothing to drink. In his frustration, he accidentally dropped the coffee pot and it broke into hundreds of little pieces all over the kitchen floor. He went to get the broom and found that mice had eaten the straw it was made from.

Just then the doorbell rang and Santa cursed on his way to the door. He opened the door and there was a little angel with a great big Christmas tree.

All radiant and smiling; the angel said, very cheerfully, "Merry Christmas Santa. Isn't it just a lovely day? I have a beautiful tree for you. Isn't it just a lovely tree? Where would you like me to stick it?"

Thus began the tradition of the little angel on top of the Christmas tree.

☺ @ ☺

All Is Not as it Seems

A woman went up to the bar in a quiet rural pub. She gestured alluringly to the bartender who approached her immediately.

She seductively signalled that he should bring his face closer to hers. As he did, she gently caressed his full beard. "Are you the manager?" she asked, softly stroking his face with both hands.

"Actually, no," he replied.

"Can you get him for me? I need to speak to him," she said, Running her hands beyond his beard and into his hair.

"I'm afraid I can't," breathed the bartender. "Is there anything I can do?"

"Yes, I need you to give him a message," she continued, running her forefinger across the bartender's lip and slyly popping a couple of her fingers into his mouth and allowing him to suck them gently.

"What should I tell him?" the bartender managed to say.

"Tell him," she whispered, "There's no toilet paper, hand soap, or paper towels in the ladies room."

☺   @   ☺

Baptising A Drunk

A man is stumbling through the woods totally drunk when he comes upon a preacher baptizing people in the river. The drunk walks into the water and subsequently bumps into the preacher. The preacher turns around and is almost overcome by the smell of booze. Whereupon he asks the drunk, 'Are you ready to find Jesus?'

'Yes I am' replies the drunk, so the preacher grabs him and dunks him in the river. He pulls him up and asks the drunk, 'Brother have you found Jesus?'

The drunk replies, 'No, I haven't.' The preacher, shocked at the answer, dunks him into the water again, but for a bit longer this time. He pulls him out of the water and asks again, 'Have you found Jesus, my brother?'

The drunk again answers, 'No, I have not found Jesus.'
By this time the preacher is at his wits end so he dunks the drunk in the water again, but this time he holds him down for about 30 seconds.

When the drunk begins kicking his arms and legs, the preacher pulls him up. The preacher asks the drunk again, 'For the love of God, have you found Jesus?'

The drunk wipes his eyes and catches his breath and says to the preacher, 'Are you sure this is where he fell in?'

☺ @ ☺

Unafraid

A few minutes before the church services started, the congregation was sitting in their pews and talking. Suddenly, Satan appeared at the front of the church.
Everyone started screaming and running for the front entrance, trampling each other in a frantic effort to get away from evil incarnate.
Soon the church was empty except for one elderly gentleman who sat calmly in his pew without moving, seemingly oblivious to the fact that God's ultimate enemy was in his presence.
So Satan walked up to the man and said, "Do you know who I am?"
The man replied, "Yep, sure do."
"Aren't you afraid of me?" Satan asked.
"Nope, sure ain't." said the man.
"Don't you realize I can kill you with one word?" asked Satan.
"Don't doubt it for a minute," returned the old man, in an even tone.
"Did you know that I can cause you profound, horrifying AGONY for all eternity?" persisted Satan.
"Yep," was the calm reply?
"And you are still not afraid?" asked Satan.
"Nope," said the old man.
More than a little perturbed, Satan asked, "Why aren't you afraid of me?"
The man calmly replied,

"Been married to your sister for 48 years

Country Doctors

A young doctor had moved out to a small community to replace a doctor who was retiring. The older doctor suggested that the young one accompany him on his rounds, so the community could become used to a new doctor. At the first house a woman complains, 'I've been a little sick to my stomach.' The older doctor says, 'Well, you've probably been overdoing the fresh fruit. Why not cut back on the amount you've been eating and see if that does the trick?'

As they left, the younger man said, 'You didn't even examine that woman. How did you come to the diagnosis so quickly?'

'I didn't have to. You noticed I dropped my stethoscope on the floor in there? When I bent over to pick it up, I noticed a half-dozen banana peels in the waste bin. That was what probably was making her sick.'

'Huh,' the younger doctor said 'Pretty clever, I think I'll try that at the next house.'

Arriving at the next house, they spent several minutes talking with a younger woman. She complained that she just didn't have the energy she once did and said, 'I'm feeling terribly run down lately .

'You've probably been doing too much work for the church,' the younger doctor told her. 'Perhaps you should cut back a bit and see if that helps.'

As they left, the elder doctor said, 'I know that woman well, your diagnosis is almost certainly correct, but how did you arrive at it?

''I did what you did at the last house, I dropped my stethoscope and when I bent down to retrieve it, noticed the vicar under the bed.'

Two Women Talking in Heaven

1st woman: Hi, I'm Sherry.
2nd woman: Hi! I'm Sylvia. How'd you die?
1st woman: I froze to death.
2nd woman: How horrible!
1st woman: It wasn't so bad. After I quit shaking from the cold, I began to get warm & sleepy, & finally died a peaceful death. What about you?
2nd woman: I died of a massive heart attack. I suspected that my husband was cheating, so I came home early to catch him in the act. But instead, I found him all by himself in the den watching TV.
1st woman: So, what happened?
2nd woman: I was so sure there was another woman there somewhere that I started running all over the house looking. I ran up into the attic & searched, & down into the basement. Then I went through every closet & checked under all the beds. I kept this up until I had looked everywhere, & finally I became so exhausted that I just keeled over with a heart attack & died.
1st woman: Too bad you didn't look in the freezer---we'd both still be alive.

☺ @ ☺

Change of Career

A gynaecologist had become fed up with malpractice insurance and NHS paperwork and was burned out.

Hoping to try another career where skilful hands would be beneficial, he decided to become an car mechanic.

He went to the local technical college, signed up for evening classes, attended diligently, and learned all he could.

When the time for the practical exam approached, the gynaecologist prepared carefully for weeks and completed the exam with tremendous skill.

When the results came back, he was surprised to find that he had obtained a score of 150%.

Fearing an error, he called the instructor, saying, "I don't want to appear ungrateful for such an outstanding result, but I wonder if there is an error in the grade."

The instructor said, "During the exam, you took the engine apart perfectly, which was worth 50% of the total mark.

"You put the engine back together again perfectly, which is also worth 50% of the mark."

After a pause, the instructor added, "I gave you an extra 50% because you did it all through the exhaust, which I've never seen done in my entire life."

☺ @ ☺

The Wisdom of Children

A little girl was talking to her teacher about whales.

The teacher said it was physically impossible for a whale to swallow a human because even though it was a very large mammal its throat was very small.

The little girl stated that Jonah was swallowed by a whale.

Irritated, the teacher reiterated that a whale could not swallow a human; it was physically impossible.

The little girl said, 'When I get to heaven I will ask Jonah'.

The teacher asked, 'What if Jonah went to hell?'

The little girl replied, 'Then you ask him'.

A Kindergarten teacher was observing her classroom of children while they were drawing.. She would occasionally walk around to see each child's work.

As she got to one little girl who was working diligently, she asked what the drawing was.

The girl replied, 'I'm drawing God.'

The teacher paused and said, 'But no one knows what God looks like.'

Without missing a beat, or looking up from her drawing, the girl replied, 'They will in a minute.'

☺ @ ☺

A Sunday school teacher was discussing the Ten Commandments with her five and six-year-olds.

After explaining the commandment to 'honour' thy Father and thy Mother, she asked, 'Is there a commandment that teaches us how to treat our brothers and sisters?'

Without missing a beat one little boy (the oldest of a family) answered, 'Thou shall not kill.'

☺ @ ☺

One day a little girl was sitting and watching her mother do the dishes at the kitchen sink. She suddenly noticed that her mother had several strands of white hair sticking out in contrast on her brunette head.

She looked at her mother and inquisitively asked, 'Why are some of your hairs white, Mum?'

Her mother replied, 'Well, every time that you do something wrong and make me cry or unhappy, one of my hairs turns white.'

The little girl thought about this revelation for a while and then said, 'Mummy, how come ALL of grandma's hairs are white?'

☺ @ ☺

The children had all been photographed, and the teacher was trying to persuade them each to buy a copy of the group picture.

'Just think how nice it will be to look at it when you are all grown up and say, 'There's Jennifer, she's a lawyer,' or 'That's Michael, he's a doctor.'

A small voice at the back of the room rang out, 'And there's the teacher, she's dead.'

☺ @ ☺

A teacher was giving a lesson on the circulation of the blood. Trying to make the matter clearer, she said, 'Now, class, if I stood on my head, the blood, as you know, would run into it, and I would turn red in the face.'

'Yes,' the class said.

'Then why is it that while I am standing upright in the ordinary position the blood doesn't run into my feet?'

A little fellow shouted,
'Cause your feet ain't empty.'

☺ @ ☺

The children were lined up in the cafeteria of a Catholic elementary school for lunch. At the head of the table was a large pile of apples. The nun made a note, and posted on the apple tray:

'Take only ONE . God is watching.'

Moving further along the lunch line, at the other end of the table was a large pile of chocolate chip cookies.

A child had written a note, 'Take all you want. God is watching the apples.'

☺   @   ☺

Yuletide Parrot Story

A young man named John received a parrot as a gift. The parrot had a bad attitude and an even worse vocabulary. Every word out of the bird's mouth was rude, obnoxious and laced with profanity.

John tried and tried to change the bird's attitude by consistently saying only polite words, playing soft music and anything else he could think of to 'clean up' the bird's vocabulary. Finally, John was fed up and he yelled at the parrot. The parrot yelled back. John shook the parrot and the parrot got angrier and even more rude.

John, in desperation, threw up his hand, grabbed the bird and put him in the freezer. For a few minutes the parrot squawked and kicked and screamed. Then suddenly there was total quiet. Not a peep was heard for over a minute.

Fearing that he'd hurt the parrot, John quickly opened the door to the freezer.

The parrot calmly stepped out onto John's outstretched arms and said, "I believe I may have offended you with my rude language and actions. I'm sincerely remorseful for my inappropriate transgressions and I fully intend to do everything I can to correct my rude and unforgivable behaviour."

John was stunned at the change in the bird's attitude. As he was about to ask the parrot what had made such a dramatic change in his behaviour, the bird spoke-up, very softly, "May I enquire what the turkey did?"

☺ @ ☺

Guess Where This is . . .

It's Viagrs'a Head Office in Toronto, Canada
Seriously – it is!

☺ @ ☺

 Before you criticize someone, you should walk a mile in their shoes. That way, when you criticize them, you're a mile away and you have their shoes.

☺ @ ☺

Taxi!

A woman and her ten-year-old son were riding in a taxi on Seymour Street in Vancouver. It was raining and all the prostitutes were standing under the awnings.

"Mum," said the boy, "what are all those women doing?"

"They're waiting for their husbands to get off work," she replied.

The taxi driver turns around and says, "Geez lady, why don't you tell him the truth? They're hookers, boy! They have sex with men for money."

The little boy's eyes get wide and he says, "Is that true, Mum?" His mother, glaring hard at the driver, answers in the affirmative.

After a few minutes, the kid asks, "Mum, what happens to the babies those women have?"

"Most of them become taxi drivers," she said.

☺   @   ☺

Careful . . .

WIFE: What would you do if I died? Would you get married again?
HUSBAND: Definitely not!
WIFE: Why not - don't you like being married?
HUSBAND: Of course I do.
WIFE: Then why wouldn't you remarry?
HUSBAND: Okay, I'd get married again.
WIFE: You would? (With a hurt look on her face).
HUSBAND: (Makes audible groan).
WIFE: Would you live in our house?
HUSBAND: Sure, it's a great house.

WIFE: Would you sleep with her in our bed?
HUSBAND: Where else would we sleep?
WIFE: Would you let her drive my car?
HUSBAND: Probably, it is almost new.
WIFE: Would you replace my pictures with hers?
HUSBAND: That would seem like the proper thing to do.
WIFE: Would she use my golf clubs?
HUSBAND: No, she's left-handed.
WIFE: - silence - -
HUSBAND: Ah . . .

☺ @ ☺

At The Races

One day while he was at the track playing the ponies and all but losing his shirt, Mitch noticed a priest who stepped out onto the track and blessed the forehead of one of the horses lining up for the 4th race. Lo and behold, that horse - a very long shot - won the race.

Before the next race, as the horses began lining up, Mitch watched with interest the old priest step onto the track. Sure enough, as the horses for the 5th race came to the starting gate the priest made a blessing on the forehead of one of the horses. Mitch made a beeline for a betting window and placed a small bet on the horse. Again, even though it was another long shot, the horse the priest had blessed won the race.

Mitch collected his winnings, and anxiously waited to see which horse the priest would bless for the 6th race. The priest again blessed a horse.

Mitch bet big on it, and it won. Mitch was elated. As the races continued the priest kept blessing long shot horses, and each one ended up coming in first.

By and by, Mitch was pulling in some serious money. By the last race, he knew his wildest dreams were going to come true. He made a quick dash to the ATM, withdrew all his savings, and awaited the priest's blessing that would tell him which horse to bet on.

True to his pattern, the priest stepped onto the track for the last race and blessed the forehead of an old nag that was the longest shot of the day.

Mitch also observed the priest blessing the eyes, ears, and hooves of the old nag. Mitch knew he had a winner and bet every cent he owned on the old nag. He then watched dumbfounded as the old nag come in dead last. Mitch, in a state of shock, made his way down to the track area where the priest was standing.

Confronting the old priest he demanded, "Father! What happened? All day long you blessed horses and they all won. Then in the last race, the horse you blessed lost by a mile. Now, thanks to you I've lost every cent of my savings - all of it."

The priest nodded wisely and with sympathy. "My son," he said, "that's the problem with you Protestants, you can't tell the difference between a simple blessing and the last rites."

☺ @ ☺

Oh Dear . . .

The police came to my door last night holding a picture of my wife.
"Is this your wife sir?" said the officer.
"Yes it is" I replied.
"I'm afraid it looks like she's been in a car accident" said the Officer...
"I know" I said, "but she has a lovely personality!"

☺ @ ☺

Court Classics

These are from a book called Disorder in the American Courts, and are things people actually said in court, taken down and now published by court reporters that had the torment of staying calm while these exchanges were actually taking place.

ATTORNEY: Are you sexually active?
WITNESS: No, I just lie there.

ATTORNEY: This myasthenia gravis, does it affect your memory at all?
WITNESS: Yes.
ATTORNEY: And in what ways does it affect your memory?
WITNESS: I forget...
ATTORNEY: You forget? Can you give us an example of something you forgot?

ATTORNEY: Now doctor, isn't it true that when a person dies in his sleep, he doesn't know about it until the next morning?
WITNESS: Did you actually pass the bar exam?

ATTORNEY: The youngest son, the 20-year-old, how old is he?
WITNESS: He's 20, much like your IQ.

ATTORNEY: Were you present when your picture was taken?
WITNESS: Are you shitting me?

ATTORNEY: So the date of conception (of the baby) was August 8th?
WITNESS: Yes.
ATTORNEY: And what were you doing at that time?

WITNESS: Getting laid.

ATTORNEY: She had three children, right?
WITNESS: Yes.
ATTORNEY: How many were boys?
WITNESS: None.
ATTORNEY: Were there any girls?
WITNESS: Your Honour, I think I need a different attorney. Can I get a new attorney?

ATTORNEY: How was your first marriage terminated?
WITNESS: By death.
ATTORNEY: And by whose death was it terminated?
WITNESS: Take a guess.

ATTORNEY: Can you describe the individual?
WITNESS: He was about medium height and had a beard.
ATTORNEY: Was this a male or a female?
WITNESS: Unless the circus was in town, I'm going with male.

ATTORNEY: Is your appearance here this morning pursuant to a deposition notice which I sent to your attorney?
WITNESS: No, this is how I dress when I go to work.

ATTORNEY: Doctor, how many of your autopsies have you performed on dead people?
WITNESS: All of them. The live ones put up too much of a fight.

ATTORNEY: ALL your responses MUST be oral, OK? What school did you go to?
WITNESS: Oral...

ATTORNEY: Do you recall the time that you examined the body?
WITNESS: The autopsy started around 8:30 pm.
ATTORNEY: And Mr. Denton was dead at the time?
WITNESS: If not, he was by the time I finished.

ATTORNEY: Are you qualified to give a urine sample?
WITNESS: Are you qualified to ask that question?

And last:

ATTORNEY: Doctor, before you performed the autopsy, did you check for a pulse?
WITNESS: No.
ATTORNEY: Did you check for blood pressure?
WITNESS: No.
ATTORNEY: Did you check for breathing?
WITNESS: No.
ATTORNEY: So, then it is possible that the patient was alive when you began the autopsy?
WITNESS: No.
ATTORNEY: How can you be so sure, Doctor?
WITNESS: Because his brain was sitting on my desk in a jar.
ATTORNEY: I see, but could the patient have still been alive, nevertheless?
WITNESS: Yes, it is possible that he could have been alive and practising law.

☺ @ ☺

Lippie

According to a news report, a certain private school in Sydney's Eastern Suburbs was recently faced with an unusual problem. A number of the girls were beginning to use lipstick and would put it on in the bathroom.

That was fine, but after they put on their lipstick they would press their lips to the mirror leaving dozens of little lip prints. Every night the maintenance man would remove them and the next day the girls would put them back.

Finally the Headmistress decided that something had to be done. She called all the girls to the bathroom and met them there with the maintenance man. She explained that all these lip prints were causing a major problem for the custodian who had to clean the mirrors every night (you can just imagine the yawns from the little princesses) .

To demonstrate how difficult it had been to clean the mirrors, she asked the maintenance man to show the girls how much effort was required.

He took out a long-handled squeegee, dipped it in the toilet bowl, and cleaned the mirror with it.

The silence was broken by a large number of gasps, a few girls vomited and apparently someone fainted. Since then there have been no lip prints on the mirror.

There are teachers . . . And then there are educators.

☺   @   ☺

Senior Banking

Shown below, is an actual letter that was sent to a bank by an 86 year old woman.   The bank manager thought it amusing enough to have it published in the New York Times.

Dear Sir:

I am writing to thank you for bouncing my check with which I endeavoured to pay my plumber last month.

By my calculations, three nanoseconds must have elapsed between his presenting the check and the arrival in my account of the funds needed to honour it..

I refer, of course, to the automatic monthly deposit of my entire pension, an arrangement which, I admit, has been in place for only eight years.

You are to be commended for seizing that brief window of opportunity, and also for debiting my account $30 by way of penalty for the inconvenience caused to your bank.

My thankfulness springs from the manner in which this incident has caused me to rethink my errant financial ways

I noticed that whereas I personally answer your telephone calls and letters, --- when I try to contact you, I am confronted by the impersonal, overcharging, pre-recorded, faceless entity which your bank has become.

From now on, I, like you, choose only to deal with a flesh-and-blood person.

My mortgage and loan repayments will therefore and hereafter no longer be automatic, but will arrive at your bank, by check, addressed personally and confidentially to an employee at your bank whom you must nominate.

Be aware that it is an OFFENCE under the Postal Act for any other person to open such an envelope.

Please find attached an Application Contact which I require your chosen employee to complete.

I am sorry it runs to eight pages, but in order that I know as much about him or her as your bank knows about me, there is no alternative.

Please note that all copies of his or her medical history must be countersigned by a Notary Public, and the mandatory details of his/her financial situation (income, debts, assets and liabilities) must be accompanied by documented proof.

In due course, at MY convenience, I will issue your employee with a PIN number which he/she must quote in dealings with me. I regret that it cannot be shorter than 28 digits but, again, I have modelled it on the number of button presses required of me to access my account balance on your phone bank service.

As they say, imitation is the sincerest form of flattery.

Let me level the playing field even further. When you call me, press buttons as follows:

IMMEDIATELY AFTER DIALLING, PRESS THE STAR (*) BUTTON FOR ENGLISH

    #1. To make an appointment to see me

    #2. To query a missing payment.

    #3. To transfer the call to my living room in case I am there.

    #4 To transfer the call to my bedroom in case I am sleeping.

    #5. To transfer the call to my toilet in case I am attending to nature.

    #6. To transfer the call to my mobile phone if I am not at home.

#7. To leave a message on my computer, a password to access my computer is required.

Your password will be communicated to you at a later date to that authorised contact mentioned earlier.

#8. To return to the main menu and to listen to options 1 through 7.

#9. To make a general complaint or inquiry. The contact will then be put on hold, pending the attention of my automated answering service.

#10. This is a second reminder to press* for English.

While this may, on occasion, involve a lengthy wait, uplifting music will play for the duration of the call.

Regrettably, but again following your example, I must also levy an establishment fee to cover the setting up of this new arrangement.

May I wish you a happy, if ever so slightly less prosperous New Year?

Your Humble Client

☺   @   ☺

Tech Support

Tech Support: What kind of computer do you have?
Customer: A white one.
....

Customer: Hi, this is Celine. I can't get my DVD out !!!
Tech Support: Have you tried pushing the button?
Customer: Yes, I'm sure it's really stuck.
Tech Support: That doesn't sound good; I'll make a note.

Customer: No, wait a minute, I hadn't inserted it yet. It's still on my desk . . . sorry. Thank you.

....

Tech Support: Click on the 'MY COMPUTER' icon on the left of the screen.
Customer: Your left or my left?

....

Tech Support: Hello. How may I help you?
Male Customer: Hi .. . . I can't print.
Tech Support: Would you click on 'START' for me and . . ....
Customer: Listen pal; don't start getting technical on me. I'm not Bill Gates!!!

....

Customer: Good afternoon, this is Martha. I can't print. Every time I try, it says . . . 'CAN'T FIND PRINTER'. I even lifted the printer and placed it in front of the monitor, but the computer still says it can't find it!!!

....

Customer: I have problems printing in red.
Tech Support: Do you have a color printer?
Customer: Aaaah . . . . thank you.

....

Tech Support: What's on your monitor now, ma'am?
Customer: A teddy bear that my boyfriend bought for me at the 7-11 store.

....

Tech Support: Your password is the small letter 'a' as in apple, a capital letter 'V' as in Victor, and the number '7'.
Customer: Is that '7' in capital letters?

....

Customer: My keyboard is not working anymore.

Tech Support: Are you sure your keyboard is plugged into the computer?
Customer: No. I can't get behind the computer.
Tech Support: Pick up your keyboard and take ten steps backwards.
Customer: Okay.
Tech Support: Did the keyboard come with you?
Customer: Yes.
Tech Support: That means the keyboard is not plugged in. Is there another keyboard?
Customer: Yes, there's another one here. Wait a moment please. . . . . . . Ah, that one does work. Thanks.

....

Customer: I can't get on the internet.
Tech Support: Are you absolutely sure you used the correct password?
Customer: Yes, I'm sure. I saw my co-worker do it.
Tech Support: Can you tell me what the password was?
Customer: Five dots.

....

Tech Support: What anti-virus program do you use?
Customer: Netscape.
Tech Support: That's not an anti-virus program.
Customer: Oh, sorry . . . Internet Explorer.

....

Customer: I have a huge problem! My friend has placed a screen saver on my computer . . . but, every time I move my mouse, it disappears.

....

Tech Support: How may I help you?
Customer: I'm writing my first email.
Tech Support: OK, and what seems to be the problem?
Customer: Well, I have the letter 'a' in the address, but how do I get the little circle around it?

A woman customer called the Canon help desk because she had a problem with her printer..
Tech Support: Are you running it under windows?
Customer: No, my desk is next to the door, but that is a good point. The man sitting next to me is by a window, and his printer is working fine!

....

And last, but not least . . .

Tech Support: Okay Bob, press the control and escape keys at the same time. That brings up a task list in the middle of the screen.. Now, type the letter 'P' to bring up the Program Manager.
Customer: I don't have a 'P'.
Tech Support: On your keyboard, Bob.
Customer: What do you mean ?
Tech Support: 'P' . . . on your keyboard, Bob.
Customer: I AM NOT GOING TO DO THAT!!!

....

☺ @ ☺

Stella Awards

It's time again for the annual Stella Awards. For those unfamiliar with these awards, they are named after 81-year-old Stella Liebeck who spilled hot coffee on herself and successfully sued a McDonald's in New Mexico , where she purchased coffee. You remember, she took the lid off the coffee and put it between her knees while she was driving. Who would ever think one could get burned doing that, right?

That's right; these are awards for the most outlandish lawsuits and verdicts in the U.S. You know, the kinds of cases that make you scratch your head and say WTF. So keep your head scratcher handy.

Here are the Stellas for the past year:
* SEVENTH PLACE *

Kathleen Robertson of Austin, Texas, was awarded $80,000 by a jury of her peers after breaking her ankle tripping over a toddler who was running inside a furniture store. The store owners were understandably surprised by the verdict, considering the running toddler was her own son.

Start scratching!

* SIXTH PLACE *

Carl Truman, 19, of Los Angeles , California , won $74,000 plus medical expenses when his neighbour ran over his hand with a Honda Accord. Truman apparently didn't notice there was someone at the wheel of the car when he was trying to steal his neighbour's hubcaps.

Scratch some more...

* FIFTH PLACE *

Terrence Dickson, of Bristol , Pennsylvania , who was leaving a house he had just burgled by way of the garage. Unfortunately for Dickson, the automatic garage door opener malfunctioned and he could not get the garage door to open. Worse, he couldn't re-enter the house because the door connecting the garage to the house locked when Dickson pulled it shut. Forced to sit for eight, count 'em, EIGHT days and survive on a case of Pepsi and a large bag of dry dog food, he sued the homeowner's insurance company claiming undue mental anguish. Amazingly, the jury said the insurance company must pay Dickson $500,000 for his anguish. We should all have this kind of anguish. Keep scratching .. There are more......

Double hand scratching after this one.....

* FOURTH PLACE *

Jerry Williams, of Little Rock, Arkansas, garnered 4th Place in the Stella's when he was awarded $14,500 plus medical expenses after being bitten on the butt by his next door neighbour's beagle - even though the beagle was on a chain in its owner's fenced yard. Williams did not get as much as he asked for because the jury believed the beagle might have been provoked at the time of the butt bite because Williams had climbed over the fence into the yard and repeatedly shot the dog with a pellet gun.

Pick a new spot to scratch, you're getting a bald spot..

* THIRD PLACE *

Amber Carson of Lancaster, Pennsylvania, because a jury ordered a Philadelphia restaurant to pay her $113,500 after she slipped on a spilled soft drink and broke her coccyx. The reason the soft drink was on the floor: Ms. Carson had thrown it at her boyfriend 30 seconds earlier during an argument.

Only two more so ease up on the scratching....

SECOND PLACE

Kara Walton, of Claymont , Delaware , sued the owner of a night club in a nearby city because she fell from the bathroom window to the floor, knocking out her two front teeth. Even though Ms.Walton was trying to sneak through the ladies room window to avoid paying the $3.50 cover charge, the jury said the night club had to pay her $12,000 ..... oh, yeah, plus dental expenses.

OK. Here we go!!

* FIRST PLACE *

This year's runaway First Place Stella Award winner was: Mrs. Merv Grazinski, of Oklahoma City, Oklahoma, who purchased new 32-foot Winnebago motor home. On her first trip home, from an OU football game, having driven on to the freeway, she set the cruise control at 70 mph and calmly left the driver's seat to go to the back of the Winnebago to make herself a sandwich. Not surprisingly, the motor home left the freeway, crashed and overturned. Also not surprisingly, Mrs. Grazinski sued Winnebago for not putting in the owner's manual that she couldn't actually leave the driver's seat while the cruise control was set. The Oklahoma jury awarded her - are you sitting down? --- $1,750,000 PLUS a new motor home. Winnebago actually changed their manuals as a result of this suit, just in case Mrs. Grazinski has any relatives who might also buy a motor home.

☺ @ ☺

When you are in deep trouble – look straight ahead, keep your mouth shut and say nothing.

Dispute Between Neighbours - this is a true story....

A city councilman in Utah, Mark Easton, had a beautiful view of the mountains to the east, until a new neighbour purchased the lot below his house and built a new home.

The new home was 18 inches higher than the ordinances would allow so Mark Easton, mad about his lost view, went to the city to make sure they enforced the lower roof line ordinance.

The new neighbour had to drop the roof line, at great expense.

Recently, Mark Easton called the city and informed them that his new neighbour had installed some vents on the side of his home...

Mark didn't like the look of these vents and asked the city to investigate.

When they went to Mark's home to see what the vents looked like, this is what they found...

The City Council said the vents can stay since there is no ordinance referring to shutter design.

☺ @ ☺

WD40

Before you read to the end, do you know what the main ingredient of WD-40 is?

I had a neighbour who had bought a new van. I got up very early one Sunday morning and saw that some vandal had spray painted red all around the sides of this white van. I went over and told him the bad news. He was very upset and was trying to work out what to do, probably nothing until Monday morning, since nothing was open.

Another neighbour came out and told him to get some WD-40 and clean it off. It removed the unwanted paint beautifully and did not harm the paint that was on the van. I'm impressed! WD-40 - how did someone work out it would do that?

'Water Displacement No.40' The product began from a search for rust preventative solvent and degreaser to protect missile parts. WD-40 was created in 1953 by three technicians at the San Diego Rocket Chemical Company. Its name comes from the project that was to find a 'water displacement' compound. They were successful with the fortieth formulation, thus WD-40. The Convair Company bought it in bulk to protect their Atlas missile parts.

Ken East (one of the original founders) says there is nothing in WD-40 that would hurt you. It's the first thing that has ever cleaned that spotty shower screen. If yours is plastic, it works just as well as on glass. It's a miracle! Then try it on your cooker top .... Kazamm! It's now shinier than it's ever been. You'll be amazed.

Here are some other uses:

1. Protects silver from tarnishing.
2. Removes road tar and grime from cars.
3. Cleans and lubricates guitar 20 strings.

4. Gives floors that 'just-waxed' sheen without making them slippery.
5. Keeps flies off cows.
6. Restores and cleans blackboards.
7. Removes lipstick stains.
8. Loosens stubborn zips.
9. Untangles jewelry chains.
10. Removes stains from stainless steel sinks.
11. Removes dirt and grime from the barbecue grill.
12. Keeps ceramic/terra cotta garden pots from oxidizing.
13. Removes tomato stains from clothing.
14. Keeps glass shower screens free of water spots.
15. Camouflages scratches in ceramic and marble floors.
16. Keeps scissors working smoothly.
17. Lubricates noisy door hinges on vehicles and doors in homes.
18. It removes black scuff marks from the kitchen floor! Use WD-40 for those nasty tar and scuff marks on flooring. It doesn't seem to harm the finish and you won't have to scrub nearly as hard to get them off. Just remember to open some windows if you have a lot of marks.
19. Dead insects will eat away the finish on your car if not removed quickly! Use WD-40!
20. Gives a children's playground gym slide a 20 shine for a super fast slide.
21. WD-40 is great for removing crayon from walls. Spray on the mark and wipe with a clean rag.
22. Also, if you've discovered that your teenage daughter has washed and dried a tube of lipstick with a load of laundry, saturate the lipstick spots with WD-40 and rewash. Presto! The lipstick is gone!
23. Lubricates tracks in sticking home windows and makes them easier to open.
24. Spraying an umbrella stem makes it easier to open and close.
25. Restores and cleans padded leather dashboards in vehicles, as well as vinyl bumpers.
26. Restores and cleans roof racks on vehicles.

27. Lubricates and stops squeaks in electric fans.
28. Lubricates wheel sprockets on tricycles, wagons, and bicycles for easy handling.
29. Lubricates fan belts on washers and dryers and keeps them running smoothly.
30. Keeps rust from forming on saws and saw blades, and other tools.
31. Removes splattered grease on stove.
32. Keeps bathroom mirror from fogging.
33. Lubricates prosthetic limbs.
34. Keeps pigeons off the balcony (they hate the smell).
35. Removes all traces of duct tape.
36. Folks even spray it on their arms, hands, and knees to relieve arthritis pain.
37. WD-40 attracts fish. Spray a little on live bait or lures and you will be catching the big one in no time. Also, it's a lot cheaper than the chemical attractants that are made for just that purpose. Keep in mind though, using some chemical laced baits or lures for fishing are not allowed in some counties .
38. Use it for gnat bites. It takes the sting away immediately and stops the itch.

And for some reason............spray it on your arthritic knee joints etc and it will ease them.

P. S. The basic ingredient is FISH OIL.
☺ @ ☺

Only The Irish

Paddy was waiting at the bus stop with his mate when a lorry went by loaded up with rolls of turf.

Paddy said, ' I gonna do that when I win lottery ' .

'What's dat ' , says his mate.

'Send me lawn away to be cut ' , says Paddy.

GOVERNMENT HEALTH WARNING:
Do Not Swallow Chewing Gum

☺ @ ☺

A Blonde goes to Heaven

A Blonde was sent on her way to Heaven. Upon arrival, a concerned St Peter met her at the Pearly Gates. 'I'm sorry, 'St Peter said; 'But Heaven is suffering from an overload of godly souls and we have been forced to put up an Entrance Exam for new arrivals to ease the burden of Heavenly Arrivals.'
'That's cool' said the Blonde, 'What does the Entrance Exam consist of?'
'Just three questions' said St Peter.
'Which are?' asked the Blonde.
'The first,' said St Peter, 'is, which two days of the week start with the letter 'T'? The second is 'How many seconds are there in a year'?
The third is 'What was the name of the swagman in Waltzing Matilda?'
'Now,' said St Peter, 'Go away and think about those questions and when I call upon you, I shall expect you to have those answers for me.'

So the Blonde went away and gave those three questions some considerable thought (I expect you to do the same).

The following morning, St Peter called upon the Blonde and asked if she had considered the questions, to which she replied, 'I have.'

'Well then,' said St Peter, 'Which two days of the week start with the letter T?'

The Blonde said, 'Today and Tomorrow.'

St Peter pondered this answer for some time, and decided that indeed the answer can be applied to the question.

'Well then, could I have your answer to the second of the three questions' St Peter went on, 'how many seconds in a year?'

The Blonde replied, 'Twelve!'

'Only twelve' exclaimed St Peter, 'How did you arrive at that figure?'

'Easy,' said the Blonde, 'there's the second of January, the second of February, right through to the second of December, giving a total of twelve seconds.'

St Peter looked at the Blonde and said, 'I need some time to consider your answer before I can give you a decision.' And he walked away shaking his head.

A short time later, St Peter returned to the Blonde. 'I'll allow the answer to stand, but you need to get the third and final question absolutely correct to be allowed into Heaven. Now, can you tell me the answer to the name of the swagman in Waltzing Matilda?'

The blonde replied: 'Of the three questions, I found this the easiest to answer.'

'Really!' exclaimed St Peter, 'And what is the answer?'

'It's Andy.'

'Andy??'

'Yes, Andy,' said the Blonde.

This totally floored St Peter, and he paced this way and that, deliberating the answer. Finally, he could not stand the suspense any longer, and turning to the blonde, asked 'How in Heaven's name did you arrive at THAT answer?'

'Easy' said the Blonde, 'Andy sat, Andy watched, Andy waited till his billy boiled.' . . . and the Blonde entered Heaven...

Indian Taxi Driver

A stark naked, drunken Australian woman, jumped into a vacant taxi in downtown New Delhi.

The Indian driver was immediately beside himself and just kept on staring at the woman. He made no attempt to start the cab.

"What's wrong with you mate, haven't you ever seen a naked white woman before?"

"I am not staring at you lady, I am telling you that would not be proper where I am coming from".

"Well if you're not bloody staring at me mate, what are you doing then?"

"Well, I am telling you, I am thinking to myself, "where is this lady keeping the money for to be paying me for the taxi fare?"

☺ @ ☺

Reply From Inland Revenue

Apparently, this is a real reply from the Inland Revenue. Your Guardian newspaper had to ask for special permission to print it. The funniest part of this is imagining the content of the letter sent to the Tax Office which prompted this reply!

Dear Mr Addison,

I am writing to you to express our thanks for your more than prompt reply to our latest communication, and also to answer some of the points you raise. I will address them, as ever, in order.

Firstly, I must take issue with your description of our last as a "begging letter". It might perhaps more properly be referred to as a "tax demand". This is how we at the Inland Revenue have always, for reasons of accuracy, traditionally referred to such documents.

Secondly, your frustration at our adding to the "endless stream of crapulent whining and panhandling vomited daily through the letterbox on to the doormat" has been noted. However, whilst I have naturally not seen the other letters to which you refer I would cautiously suggest that their being from "pauper councils, Lombardy pirate banking houses and pissant gas-mongerers" might indicate that your decision to "file them next to the toilet in case of emergencies" is at best a little ill-advised. In common with my own organisation, it is unlikely that the senders of these letters do see you as a "lackwit bumpkin" or, come to that, a "sodding charity". More likely they see you as a citizen of Great Britain, with a responsibility to contribute to the upkeep of the nation as a whole.

Which brings me to my next point. Whilst there may be some spirit of truth in your assertion that the taxes you pay "go to shore up the canker-blighted, toppling folly that is the Public Services", a moment's rudimentary calculation ought to disabuse you of the notion that the government in any way expects you to "stump up for the whole damned party" yourself. The estimates you provide for the Chancellor's disbursement of the funds levied by taxation, whilst colourful, are, in fairness, a little off the mark. Less than you seem to imagine is spent on "junkets for Bunterish lickspittles" and "dancing whores" whilst far more than you have accounted for is allocated to, for example, "that box-ticking facade of a university system."

A couple of technical points arising from direct queries:

1. The reason we don't simply write "Muggins" on the envelope has to do with the vagaries of the postal system.

2. You can rest assured that "sucking the very marrow of those with nothing else to give" has never been considered as a practice because even if the Personal Allowance didn't render it irrelevant, the sheer medical logistics involved would make it financially unviable.

I trust this has helped. In the meantime, whilst I would not in any way wish to influence your decision one way or the other, I ought to point out that even if you did choose to "give the whole foul jamboree up and go and live in India" you would still owe us the money.

Please send it to us by Friday..

Yours sincerely,
H J Lee
Customer Relations
Inland Revenue

☺ @ ☺

DC airline reservation agent offers some examples of 'why' their country is in trouble:

1. I had a New Hampshire Congresswoman (Carol Shea-Porter) ask for an aisle seat so that her hair wouldn't get messed up by being near the window. (On an aeroplane!)

2. I got a call from a Kansas Congressman's (Moore) staffer (Howard Bauleke), who wanted to go to Capetown. I started to explain the length of the flight and the passport information, and then he interrupted me with, "I'm not trying to make you look stupid, but Capetown is in Massachusetts .."

Without trying to make him look stupid, I calmly explained, "Cape Cod is in Massachusetts , Capetown is in Africa "

His response -- click.

3. A senior Vermont Congressman (Bernie Sanders) called, furious about a Florida package we did. I asked what was wrong with the vacation in Orlando. He said he was expecting an ocean-view room. I tried to explain that's not possible, since Orlando is in the middle of the state.

He replied, 'don't lie to me, I looked on the map and Florida is a very thin state!" (OMG)

4. I got a call from a lawmaker's wife (Landra Reid) who asked, "Is it possible to see England from Canada ?"

I said, "No."

She said, "But they look so close on the map." (OMG, again!)

5. An aide for a cabinet member(Janet Napolitano) once called and asked if he could rent a car in Dallas. I pulled up the reservation and noticed he had only a 1-hour layover in Dallas. When I asked him why he wanted to rent a car, he said, "I heard Dallas was a big airport, and we will need a car to drive between gates to save time." (Aghhhh)

6. An Illinois Congresswoman (Jan Schakowsky) called last week. She needed to know how it was possible that her flight from Detroit left at 8:30 a.m., and got to Chicago at 8:33 a.m. I explained that Michigan was an hour ahead of Illinois, but she couldn't understand the concept of time zones. Finally, I told her the plane went fast, and she bought that.

7. A New York lawmaker, (Jerrold Nadler) called and asked, "Do airlines put your physical description on your bag so they know whose luggage belongs to whom?" I said, 'No, why do you ask?'

He replied, "Well, when I checked in with the airline, they put a tag on my luggage that said (FAT), and I'm overweight. I think that's very rude!"

After putting him on hold for a minute, while I looked into it. (I was dying laughing). I came back and explained the city code for Fresno, Ca. Is (FAT - Fresno Air Terminal), and the airline was just putting a destination tag on his luggage.

8. A Senator John Kerry aide (Lindsay Ross) called to inquire about a trip package to Hawaii. After going over all the cost info, she asked, "Would it be cheaper to fly to California and then take the train to Hawaii?"

9. I just got off the phone with a freshman Congressman, Bobby Bright (D) from Alabama who asked, "How do I know which plane to get on?"

I asked him what exactly he meant, to which he replied, "I was told my flight number is 823, but none of these planes have numbers on them."

10. Senator Dianne Feinstein (D) called and said, "I need to fly to Pepsi-Cola, Florida. Do I have to get on one of those little computer planes?"

I asked if she meant fly to Pensacola, FL on a commuter plane.

She said, "Yeah, whatever, smarty!"

11. Mary Landrieu (D) La. Senator called and had a question about the documents she needed in order to fly to China. After a lengthy discussion about passports, I reminded her that she needed a visa. 'Oh, no I don't. I've been to China many times and never had to have one of those.'

I double checked and sure enough, her stay required a visa. When I told her this she said, "Look, I've been to China four times and every time they have accepted my American Express!"

12. A New Jersey Congressman (John Adler) called to make reservations, "I want to go from Chicago to Rhino, New York."

I was at a loss for words. Finally, I said, "Are you sure that's the name of the town?"

'Yes, what flights do you have?" replied the man.

After some searching, I came back with, "I'm sorry, sir, I've looked up every airport code in the country and can't find a rhino anywhere."

"The man retorted, "Oh, don't be silly! Everyone knows where it is. Check your map!"

So I scoured a map of the state of New York and finally offered, "You don't mean Buffalo, do you?"

The reply? "Whatever! I knew it was a big animal."

☺ @ ☺

New Website

In the not too distant future, YouTube, Twitter & Facebook will merge to form one giant, idiotic, super, time-wasting website called ...

You twitface

☺ @ ☺

Police Complaint

This is a allegedly a genuine complaint to Greenock Police Force from an angry member of the public.

Dear Sir/Madam,

Re: Automated telephone answering service:

Having spent the past twenty minutes waiting for someone at Greenock police station to pick up a telephone I have decided to abandon the idea and try e-mailing you instead.

Perhaps you would be so kind as to pass this message on to your colleagues in Greenock , by means of smoke signal, carrier pigeon or Ouija board.

As I'm writing this e-mail there are eleven failed medical experiments (I think you call them youths) in Mathie Crescent, which is just off Mathie Road in Gourock.

Six of them seem happy enough to play a game which involves kicking a football against an iron gate with the force of a meteorite. This causes an earth shattering CLANG! which rings throughout the entire building. This game is now in its third week and as I am unsure how the scoring system works, I have no idea if it will end any time soon.

The remaining five failed-abortions are happily rummaging through several bags of rubbish and items of furniture that someone has so thoughtfully dumped beside the wheelie bins. One of them has found a saw and is setting about a discarded chair like a beaver on ecstasy pills.

I fear that it's only a matter of time before they turn their limited attention to the caravan gas bottle that is lying on its side between the two bins.

If they could be relied on to only blow their own arms and legs off then I would happily leave them to it. I would even go so far as to lend them the matches. Unfortunately they are far more likely to blow up half the street with them and I've just finished decorating the kitchen.

What I suggest is this - after replying to this e-mail with worthless assurances that the matter is being looked into and will be dealt with, why not leave it until the one night of the year (probably bath night) when there are no mutants around then drive up the street in a Panda car before doing a three point turn and disappearing again. This will of course serve no other purpose than to remind us what policemen actually look like.

I trust that when I take a claw hammer to the skull of one of these throwbacks you'll do me the same courtesy of giving me a four month head start before coming to arrest me.

I remain your obedient servant
???????

Mr ??????,

I have read your e-mail and understand your frustration at the problems caused by youths playing in the area and the problems you have encountered in trying to contact the police.

As the Community Beat Officer for your street I would like to extend an offer of discussing the matter fully with you. Should you wish to discuss the matter, please provide contact details (address / telephone number) and when may be suitable.

Regards
PC ???????
Community Beat Officer

Dear PC ???????

First of all I would like to thank you for the speedy response to my original e-mail. 16 hours and 38 minutes must be a personal record for Greenock Police Station, and rest assured that I will forward these details to Norris McWhirter for inclusion in his next Guinness book. Secondly I was delighted to hear that our street has its own Community Beat Officer.

May I be the first to congratulate you on your covert skills? In the five or so years I have lived in Mathie Crescent , I have never seen you. Do you hide up a tree or have you gone deep undercover and infiltrated the gang itself? Are you the one with the acne and the moustache on his forehead or the one with a chin like a wash hand basin? It's surely only a matter of time before you are head-hunted by MI5 to look for Osama.

Whilst I realise that there may be far more serious crimes taking place in Gourock, such as smoking in a public place or being Christian without due care and attention, is it too much to ask for a policeman to explain (using words of no more than two syllables at a time) to these twats that they might want to play their strange football game elsewhere?

The pitch on Larkfield Road or the one at Battery Park are both within spitting distance, as is the bottom of the Gourock Dock, the latter being the preferred option especially if the tide is in.

Should you wish to discuss these matters further you should feel free to contact me on <???????>. If after 25 minutes I have still failed to answer, I'll buy you a large one in Monty's Pub.

Regards
?????????

P.S If you think that this is sarcasm, think yourself lucky that you don't work for the sewerage department with whom I am also in contact!

The Trap

The husband and his young wife were not on good terms. In fact the wife was convinced that he was carrying on with the pretty housemaid, so she laid a trap.

One Friday afternoon she sent the housemaid home for the weekend, and didn't tell her husband.

That night when they went to bed, the husband gave the old story: "Excuse me my dear, my stomach," and disappeared towards the bathroom.

The wife promptly dashed along the corridor, up the back stairs, into the maid's bed. She just had time to switch the lights off when in he came silently.

He wasted no time or words but quickly undid his trousers, and got on top of her. When he finished and still panting, the wife said "You didn't expect to find me in this bed did you!!" and switched on the light.

"No, madam", said the gardener.

☺ @ ☺

Dangerous Food

A doctor was addressing a large audience in Oxford …

"The material we put into our stomachs should have killed most of us sitting here, years ago. Red meat is full of steroids and dye. Soft drinks corrode your stomach lining. Chinese food is loaded with MSG. High transfat diets can be disastrous and none of us realizes the long-term harm caused by the germs in our drinking water.

But, there is one thing that is the most dangerous of all and most of us have, or will eat it.

Can anyone here tell me what food it is that causes the most grief and suffering for years after eating it?"

After several seconds of quiet, a 70-year-old man in the front row raised his hand, and softly said, "Wedding Cake."

☺ @ ☺

Tap on the Shoulder ....

A true story from the pages of the Manchester Evening Times.

Last Wednesday a passenger in a taxi heading for Salford station leaned over to ask the driver a question and gently tapped him on the shoulder to get his attention.

The driver screamed, lost control of the cab, nearly hit a bus, drove up over the curb and stopped just inches from a large plate window. For a few moments everything was silent in the cab. Then, the shaking driver said. "Are you OK? I'm so sorry, but you scared the daylights out of me."

The badly shaken passenger apologized to the driver and said, "I didn't realize that a mere tap on the shoulder would startle someone so badly."

The driver replied, "No, no, I'm the one who is sorry, it's entirely my fault. Today is my very first day driving a cab. I've been driving a hearse for 25 years."

☺ @ ☺

A mate of mine recently admitted to being addicted to brake fluid. When I quizzed him on it he reckoned he could stop any time....

Ten Best Caddy Remarks

#10   Golfer: "Think I'm going to drown myself in the lake."
   Caddy: "Think you can keep your head down that long?"

#9   Golfer: "I'd move heaven and earth to break 100 on this course."
   Caddy: "Try heaven, you've already moved most of the earth."

#8   Golfer: "Do you think my game is improving?"
   Caddy: "Yes, you miss the ball much closer now."

#7   Golfer: "Do you think I can get there with a 5 iron?"
   Caddy: "Eventually."

#6   Golfer: "You've got to be the worst caddy in the world."
   Caddy: "I don't think so. That would be too much of a coincidence."

#5   Golfer: "Please stop checking your watch all the time. It's too much of a distraction."
   Caddy: "It's not a watch - it's a compass."

#4   Golfer: "How do you like my game?"
   Caddy: "Very good, but personally, I prefer golf."

#3   Golfer: "Do you think it's a sin to play on Sunday?"
   Caddy: "The way you play, it's a sin on any day."

#2   Golfer: "This is the worst course I've ever played on."
   Caddy: "This isn't the golf course. We left that an hour ago."

#1 Best Caddy Comment:
   Golfer: "That can't be my ball, it's too old."
   Caddy: "It's been a long time since we teed off, sir.."

☺ @ ☺

NEW BOOK ON "HOW TO UNDERSTAND WOMEN"

☺   @   ☺

Out of the Mouths . .

JACK (age 3) was watching his Mom breast-feeding his new baby sister. After a while he asked: "Mom why have you got two? Is one for hot and one for cold milk?"

MELANIE (age 5) asked her Granny how old she was. Granny replied she was so old she didn't remember any more. Melanie said, "If you don't remember you must look in the back of your panties. Mine say five to six."

STEVEN (age 3) hugged and kissed his Mum good night. 'I love you so much that when you die I'm going to bury you outside my bedroom window.'

BRITTANY (age 4) had an ear ache and wanted a pain killer. She tried in vain to take the lid off the bottle. Seeing her frustration, her Mum explained it was a child-proof cap and she'd have to open it for her. Eyes wide with wonder, the little girl asked: 'How does it know it's me?'

SUSAN (age 4) was drinking juice when she got the hiccups. 'Please don't give me this juice again,' she said, 'It makes my teeth cough.'

DJ (age 4) stepped onto the bathroom scale and asked: 'How much do I cost?'

CLINTON (age 5) was in his bedroom looking worried When his Mum asked what was troubling him, he replied, 'I don't know what'll happen with this bed when I get married. How will my wife fit in it?'

MARC (age 4) was engrossed in a young couple that were hugging and kissing in a restaurant. Without taking his eyes off them, he asked his dad: 'Why is he whispering in her mouth?'

TAMMY (age 4) was with her mother when they met an elderly, rather wrinkled woman her Mum knew. Tammy looked at her for a while and then asked, 'Why doesn't your skin fit your face?'

JAMES (age 4) was listening to a Bible story. His dad read: 'The man named Lot was warned to take his wife and flee out of the city but his wife looked back and was turned to salt.' Concerned, James asked: 'What happened to the flea?'

'Dear Lord,' the minister began, with arms extended toward heaven and a rapturous look on his upturned face 'Without you, we are but dust....' He would have continued but at that moment my very obedient daughter who was listening leaned over to me and asked quite audibly in her shrill little four year old girl voice, 'Mum, what is butt dust?'

Quick Thinking

An elderly man had owned a large farm for several years. He had a large pond in the back.

It was properly shaped for swimming, so he fixed it up with picnic tables, and some orange, and lime trees.

One evening the old farmer decided to go down to the pond, as he hadn't been there for a while, and look it over. He grabbed a five-gallon bucket to bring back some fruit.

As he neared the pond, he heard voices shouting and laughing with glee. As he came closer, he saw it was a bunch of young women skinny-dipping in his pond.

He made the women aware of his presence and they all swam to the deep end.

One of the women shouted to him, 'We're not coming out until you leave!'

The old man grinned, 'I didn't come down here to watch you ladies swim naked or make you get out of the pond'

Holding the bucket up he said, 'I'm here to feed the alligator.'

☺ @ ☺

The Shredder

A young engineer was leaving the office at 5.45 p.m. When he found the boss standing in front of the shredder with a piece of paper in his hand.

"Listen," said the boss, "This is a very sensitive and important document. And my secretary is not here. Can you make this thing work?"

"Certainly." said the employee. He turned on the machine, and inserted the sheet of paper and pressed the button.

"Excellent, excellent." said the boss as the paper disappeared inside the machine. " I just need the one copy."

Lesson: Never, never assume that your boss knows what he's doing.

☺ @ ☺

Cat Washing

This is simply too much of a time saver not to share it with you!

1. Put both lids of the toilet up and add 1/8 cup of pet shampoo to the water in the bowl.

2. Pick up the cat and soothe him while you carry him towards the bathroom..

3. In one smooth movement put the cat in the toilet and close the lid. You may need to stand on the lid.

4. The cat will self agitate and make ample suds. Never mind the noises that come from the toilet, the cat is actually enjoying this.

5. Flush the toilet three or four times, this provides a 'power-wash and rinse'.

6. Have someone open the front door of your home. Be sure that there are no people between the bathroom and the front door.

7. Stand behind the toilet as far as you can, and quickly lift the lid.

8. The cat will rocket out of the toilet, streak through the bathroom, and run outside where he will dry himself off.

9. Both the toilet and the cat will be sparkling clean.

☺ @ ☺

The Irish Priest

An Irish priest was transferred to Boonah. Father O'Malley rose from his bed one morning.

It was a fine spring day in his new parish. He walked to the window of his bedroom to get a deep breath of the beautiful day outside. He then noticed there was a donkey lying dead in the middle of his front lawn.

He promptly called the local police station......

The conversation went like this: "Good morning. This is Sergeant Tierney. How might I help you?"

"And the best of the day te yerself. This is Father O'Malley at the Church. There's a donkey lying dead on me front lawn."

Sergeant Tierney, considering himself to be quite a wit, replied with a smirk, "Well now Father, it was always my impression that you people took care of the last rites!"

There was dead silence on the line for a moment ....

Father O'Malley then replied: 'Aye, 'tis certainly true; but we are also obliged to notify the next of kin."

☺ @ ☺

Children were asked questions about the Old and New Testaments. . .

1. In the first Book of The Bible, Guinnessis, God got tired of creating the world so he took the Sabbath off.

2. Adam and Eve were created from an apple tree, Noah's wife was Joan of Ark. Noah built an ark and the animals came on in pears.

3. Lot's wife was a pillar of salt during the day, but a ball of fire during the night.

4. The Jews were a proud people and throughout history they had trouble with unsympathetic genitals.

5. Sampson was a strongman who let himself be led astray by a Jezebel like Delilah.

6. Samson slayed the Philistines with the Axe of the Apostles.

7. Moses led the Jews to the Red Sea where they made unleavened bread which is bread without any ingredients.

8. The Egyptians were all drowned in the dessert. Afterwards Moses went up Mount Cyanide to get the Ten Commandments.

9. The First Commandment was when Eve told Adam to eat the apple.

10. The Seventh Commandment is thou shalt not admit adultery.

11. Moses died before he ever reached Canada. . Then Joshua led the Hebrews in the Battle of Geritol.

12. The greatest miracle in the Bible is when Joshua told his son to stand still and he obeyed him.

13. David was a Hebrew king who was skilled at playing the liar. He fought the Finkelsteins, a race of people who lived in Biblical times.

14. Solomon, one of David's sons, had 300 wives and 700 porcupines.

15. When Mary heard she was the mother of Jesus, she sang the Magna Carta.

16. When the three wise guys from the East Side arrived they found Jesus in the manager.

17. Jesus was born because Mary had an immaculate contraption.

18. St. John , the blacksmith, dumped water on his head.

19. The people who followed the Lord were called the 12 Decibels

20. The Epistels were the wives of the Apostles.

21. Christians have only one spouse. This is called monotony.

☺ @ ☺

Japanese Banks in Crisis Again

Following the problems in the Eurozone, uncertainty has once again hit Japan. In the last 7 days Origami Bank has folded, Sumo Bank has gone belly up and Bonsai Bank announced plans to cut some of its branches.

Yesterday, it was announced that Karaoke Bank is up for sale and will likely go for a song while today shares in Kamikaze Bank were suspended after they nose-dived.

Samurai Bank are soldiering on following sharp cutbacks and Ninja Bank are reported to have taken a hit, but they remain in the black.

Fuji Bank has a mountain to climb if they are to survive this crisis and the statements from the Sudoku bank have been really quite puzzling.

Furthermore, 500 staff at Karate Bank got the chop and analysts report that there is something fishy going on at Sushi Bank where it is feared that staff may get a raw deal.

☺ @ ☺

Uh-Oh

Wife comes home late at night and quietly opens the door to her bedroom. From under the blanket she sees four legs instead of two. She reaches for a Baseball Bat and starts hitting the blanket as hard as she can. Once she's done, with a sense of pride and satisfaction she goes to the kitchen to have a drink.

As she enters, she sees her husband there, reading a magazine.

" Hi darling" he says. " Your parents have come to visit us, so I let them stay in our bedroom. Hope you have said Hello to them."

Winner – Wet T-Shirt Contest

☺ @ ☺

Don't Get Ill in Glasgow

These are sentences exactly as typed by medical secretaries in NHS Greater Glasgow

1. The patient has no previous history of suicide.
2. Patient has left her white blood cells at another hospital.
3. Patient's medical history has been remarkably insignificant with only a 40 pound weight gain in the past three days.
4. She has no rigors or shaking chills, but her husband states she was very hot in bed last night.
5. Patient has chest pain if she lies on her left side for over a year.
6. On the second day the knee was better and on the third day it disappeared.
7. The patient is tearful and crying constantly. She also appears to be depressed.
8. The patient has been depressed since she began seeing me in 1993.

9. Discharge status: Alive, but without my permission.
10. Healthy appearing decrepit 69-year old male, mentally alert, but forgetful.
11. Patient had waffles for breakfast and anorexia for lunch.
12. She is numb from her toes down.
13. While in ER, she was examined, x-rated and sent home.
14. The skin was moist and dry.
15. Occasional, constant infrequent headaches.
16. Patient was alert and unresponsive.
17. Rectal examination revealed a normal size thyroid.
18. She stated that she had been constipated for most of her life until she got a divorce.
19. I saw your patient today, who is still under our care for physical therapy.
20. Both breasts are equal and reactive to light and accommodation.
21. Examination of genitalia reveals that he is circus sized.
22. The lab test indicated abnormal lover function.
23. Skin: somewhat pale, but present.
24. The pelvic exam will be done later on the floor.
25. Large brown stool ambulating in the hall.
26. Patient has two teenage children, but no other abnormalities.
27. When she fainted, her eyes rolled around the room.
28. The patient was in his usual state of good health until his aeroplane ran out of fuel and crashed.
29. Between you and me, we ought to be able to get this lady pregnant.
30. She slipped on the ice and apparently her legs went in separate directions in early December.
31. Patient was seen in consultation by Dr. Smith, who felt we should sit on the abdomen and I agree.
32. The patient was to have a bowel resection. However, he took a job as a stock broker instead.
33. By the time he was admitted, his rapid heart had stopped, and he was feeling better.

☺ @ ☺

A Cowboy's Tombstone

Here are the Five Rules for Men to Follow for a Happy Life that Russell J. Larsen had inscribed on his headstone in Logan, Utah. He died not knowing that he would win the "Coolest Headstone" contest.

FIVE RULES FOR MEN TO FOLLOW FOR A HAPPY LIFE:

1. It's important to have a woman who helps at home, cooks from time to time, cleans up, and has a job.

2. It's important to have a woman who can make you laugh.

3. It's important to have a woman who you can trust, and doesn't lie to you.

4. It's important to have a woman who is good in bed, and likes to be with you.

5. It's very, very important that these four women do not know each other or you could end up dead like me.

☺ @ ☺

Clever

If you're not familiar with the work of Steven Wright, he's the famous Erudite (comic) scientist who once said: "I woke up one morning, and all of my stuff had been stolen and replaced by exact duplicates." His mind sees things differently than most of us do. . ..

Here are some of his gems:

1 - I'd kill for a Nobel Peace Prize.
2 - Borrow money from pessimists -- they don't expect it back.
3 - Half the people you know are below average.
4 - 99% of lawyers give the rest a bad name.
5 - 82.7% of all statistics are made up on the spot.
6 - A conscience is what hurts when all your other parts feel so good.
7 - A clear conscience is usually the sign of a bad memory.
8 - If you want the rainbow, you have to put up with the rain.
9 - All those who believe in psycho kinesis, raise my hand.
10 - The early bird may get the worm, but the second mouse gets the cheese.
11 - I almost had a psychic girlfriend, ... but she left me before we met.
12 - OK, so what's the speed of dark?
13 - How do you tell when you're out of invisible ink?
14 - If everything seems to be going well, you have obviously overlooked something.
15 - Depression is merely anger without enthusiasm.
16 - When everything is coming your way, you're in the wrong lane.
17 - Ambition is a poor excuse for not having enough sense to be lazy.
18 - Hard work pays off in the future; laziness pays off now.
19 - I intend to live forever... So far, so good.
20 - If Barbie is so popular, why do you have to buy her friends?
21 - Eagles may soar, but weasels don't get sucked into jet engines.

22 - What happens if you get scared half to death twice?
23 - My mechanic told me, "I couldn't repair your brakes, so I made your horn louder."
24 - Why do psychics have to ask you for your name.
25 - If at first you don't succeed, destroy all evidence that you tried.
26 - A conclusion is the place where you got tired of thinking.
27 - Experience is something you don't get until just after you need it.
28 - The hardness of the butter is proportional to the softness of the bread.
29 - The problem with the gene pool is that there is no lifeguard.
30 - The sooner you fall behind, the more time you'll have to catch up.
31 - The colder the x-ray table, the more of your body is required to be on it.
32 - Everyone has a photographic memory; some just don't have film.
33 - If at first you don't succeed, skydiving is not for you.
34 - If your car could travel at the speed of light, would your headlights work?

☺ @ ☺

Today's Stock Market Report

Helium was up, feathers were down. Paper was stationary.
Fluorescent tubing was dimmed in light trading. Knives were up sharply.
Cows steered into a bull market. Pencils lost a few points. Hiking equipment was trailing.
Elevators rose, while escalators continued their slow decline.
Weights were up in heavy trading.
Light switches were off.
Mining equipment hit rock bottom. Nappies remain unchanged.

☺ @ ☺

MPs

While walking down the street one day a "Member of Parliament" is tragically hit by a truck and dies. His soul arrives in heaven and is met by St. Peter at the entrance.

'Welcome to heaven,' says St. Peter. 'Before you settle in, it seems there is a problem. We seldom see a high official around these parts, you see, so we're not sure what to do with you.'

'No problem, just let me in,' says the man.

'Well, I'd like to, but I have orders from higher up. What we'll do is have you spend one day in hell and one in heaven. Then you can choose where to spend eternity.'

'Really, I've made up my mind. I want to be in heaven,' says the MP.

'I'm sorry, but we have our rules.'

And with that, St. Peter escorts him to the elevator and he goes down, down, down to hell. The doors open and he finds himself in the middle of a green golf course. In the distance is a clubhouse and standing in front of it are all his friends and other politicians who had worked with him.

Everyone is very happy and in evening dress. They run to greet him, shake his hand, and reminisce about the good times they had while getting rich at the expense of the people. They play a friendly game of golf and then dine on lobster, caviar and champagne.

Also present is the devil, who really is a very friendly and nice guy who has a good time dancing and telling jokes. They are having such a good time that before he realizes it, it is time to go.

Everyone gives him a hearty farewell and waves while the elevator rises. The elevator goes up, up, up and the door reopens on heaven where St. Peter is waiting for him.

'Now it's time to visit heaven.'

So, 24 hours pass with the MP joining a group of contented souls moving from cloud to cloud, playing the harp and singing. They have a good time and, before he realizes it, the 24 hours have gone by and St. Peter returns.

'Well, then, you've spent a day in hell and another in heaven. Now choose your eternity.'

The MP reflects for a minute, then he answers: 'Well, I would never have said it before, I mean heaven has been delightful, but I think I would be better off in hell.'

So St. Peter escorts him to the elevator and he goes down, down, down to hell. Now the doors of the elevator open and he's in the middle of a barren land covered with waste and garbage. He sees all his friends, dressed in rags, picking up the trash and putting it in black bags as more trash falls from above.

The devil comes over to him and puts his arm around his shoulder. 'I don't understand,' stammers the MP.' 'Yesterday I was here and there was a golf course and clubhouse, and we ate lobster and caviar, drank champagne, and danced and had a great time. Now there's just a wasteland full of garbage and my friends look miserable.

What happened? '

The devil looks at him, smiles and says, 'Yesterday we were campaigning. Today you voted.'

☺   @   ☺

Great Put Down

A bloke had an appointment to see the urologist who shared offices with several other doctors. The waiting room was filled with patients.

As he approached the receptionist's desk, he noticed that the receptionist was a large unfriendly woman who looked like a Sumo wrestler.

He gave her his name.

In a very loud voice, the receptionist said, "YES, I HAVE YOUR NAME HERE; YOU WANT TO SEE THE DOCTOR ABOUT IMPOTENCE, RIGHT?"

All the patients in the waiting room snapped their heads around to look at the very embarrassed Donnie.

He recovered quickly, and in an equally loud voice replied, "NO. I'VE COME TO ENQUIRE ABOUT A SEX CHANGE OPERATION, BUT I DON'T WANT THE SAME DOCTOR THAT DID YOURS."

The room erupted in applause.

☺ @ ☺

Last Wishes

Edinburgh man Willie McTavish is on his deathbed and knows the end is near. Present is the nurse, his wife, his daughter and his two sons.

Willie raises his head from his pillow and slowly speaks...

"Bernie" he says, "I want you to take the Braid Hills houses."

"Sybil, take the flats over in Morningside and Bruntsfield."

" Tam, I want you to take the offices in Charlotte Square."

"Sarah, my dear wife, please take all the residential buildings in the New Town."

The nurse is just blown away by all this and, as Willie quietly slips away, she says, "Mrs. McTavish, your husband must have been such a hard-working man to have accumulated all this property".

Sarah replies, "Property... the silly old fool has a paper round!"

☺   @   ☺

Stunt Pilot

A young girl walks into a supermarket and on her way round she sees the bloke who had his wicked way with her the previous evening, after they had met in a pub. He was stacking washing powder boxes on the shelves.

 "You lying toad" she yells" last night you told me you were a stunt pilot"

"No" he says "I told you I was a member of the Ariel display team"

☺   @   ☺

The Way Women Think

Husband's Message (by cellphone):

"Honey, I got hit by a car outside of the office. Paula brought me to the Hospital. They have been making tests and taking X-rays. The blow to my head though very strong, will not have any serious or lasting injury.

But, I have three broken ribs, a broken arm, a compound fracture in the left leg, and they may have to amputate the right foot."

Wife's Response:

"Who the Hell is Paula?"

☺ @ ☺

Testicle Therapy

Two women were playing golf. One teed off and watched in horror as her ball headed directly toward a foursome of men playing the next hole.

The ball hit one of the men. He immediately clasped his hands together at his groin, fell to the ground and proceeded to roll around in agony. The woman rushed down to the man, and immediately began to apologize. "Please allow me to help. I'm a Physical Therapist and I know I could relieve your pain if you'd allow me." she told him.

"Oh, no, I'll be all right. I'll be fine in a few minutes." the man replied. He was in obvious agony, lying in the foetal position, still clasping his hands at his groin. At her persistence, however, he finally allowed her to help.

She gently took his hands away and laid them to the side, loosened his pants and put her hands inside.

She administered tender and artful massage for several long moments and asked, "How does that feel?"

"Feels great," he replied; "but I still think my thumb's broken!"

☺ @ ☺

☺ @ ☺

Hair in Dog's Ears

My neighbour found out that her dog could hardly hear, so she took it to the veterinarian. The vet found that the problem was hair in the dog's ears. He cleaned both ears, and the dog could hear fine. The vet then proceeded to tell the lady that, if she wanted to keep this from recurring, she should go to the chemist and get some "Nair" hair remover and rub it in the dog's ears once a month.

The lady went to the chemist and bought some "Nair" hair remover. At the register, the pharmacist told her, "If you're going to use this under your arms, don't use deodorant for a few days."

The lady said, "I'm not using it under my arms."

The pharmacist said, "If you're using it on your legs, don't shave for a couple of days."

The lady replied, "I'm not using it on my legs either. If you must know, I'm using it on my schnauzer."

The pharmacist said, "Stay off your bicycle for about a week."

☺ @ ☺

Groups of Americans were travelling by tour bus through Switzerland . As they stopped at a cheese farm, a young guide led them through the process of cheese making, explaining that goat's milk was used. She showed the group a lovely hillside where many goats were grazing.

'These,' she explained, 'are the older goats put out to pasture when they no longer produce.' She then asked, 'What do you do in America with your old goats?' A spry old gentleman answered, 'They send us on bus tours!'

☺ @ ☺

NURSE

A man goes to the clinic and is seen by a nurse. He is a bit embarrassed as he was expecting to see a male doctor. He says to the nurse: "If I discuss this with you will you please not laugh at me."

"Of course I won't laugh, I'm a professional nurse. In over twenty years I've never laughed at a patient."

"Okay then," Fred said and proceeded to drop his trousers, revealing the tiniest man thingy the nurse had ever seen. Length and width, it couldn't have been bigger than a AAA battery.

Unable to control herself, the nurse started giggling then fell around laughing. She was at last able to struggle to regain her composure.

"I'm so sorry," said the nurse. "I don't know what came over me. On my honour as a nurse and a lady, I promise it won't happen again. Now, tell me, what seems to be the problem?"

"It's very swollen," Fred replied.

☺   @   ☺

CHILD TAKES A PICTURE TO SCHOOL:

After it was marked and the child brought it home, she returned to school the next day with the following note:

Dear Ms. Davis,

I want to be very clear on my child's illustration. It is NOT of me on a dance pole on a stage in a strip joint. I work at B&Q and had commented to my daughter how much money we made in the recent snowstorm. This photo is of me selling a shovel.

Mrs. Harrington

TRAVELLING TO AUSTRALIA?

These were posted on an Australian tourism website, and the answers are the actual responses by the website officials, who obviously have a great sense of humor (not to mention a low tolerance threshold for cretins!)

Q: Does it ever get windy in Australia ? I have never seen it rain on TV, how do the plants grow? (UK).
A: We import all plants fully grown, and then just sit around watching them die.

Q: Will I be able to see kangaroos in the street? (USA)
A: Depends how much you've been drinking.

Q: I want to walk from Perth to Sydney - can I follow the railroad tracks? (Sweden)
A: Sure, it's only three thousand miles. Take lots of water.

Q: Are there any ATMs (cash machines) in Australia? Can you send me a list of them in Brisbane, Cairns, Townsville and Hervey Bay? (UK)
A: What did your last slave die of?

Q: Can you give me some information about hippo racing in Australia? (USA)
A: Af-ri-ca is the big triangle shape continent south of Europe . Aust-ra-lia is that big island in the middle of the Pacific which does not ...
Oh, forget it. Sure, the hippo racing is every Tuesday night in Kings Cross. Come naked.

Q: Which direction is North in Australia? (USA)
A: Face south, and then turn 180 degrees. Contact us when you get here and we'll send the rest of the directions.

Q: Can I bring cutlery into Australia? (UK)
A: Why? Just use your fingers like we do.

Q: Can you send me the Vienna Boys' Choir schedule? (USA)
A: Aus-tri-a is that quaint little country bordering Ger-man-y, which is ...
Oh, forget it. Sure, the Vienna Boys Choir plays every Tuesday night in Kings Cross, straight after the hippo races. Come naked.

Q: Can I wear high heels in Australia? (UK)
A: You are a British politician, right?

Q: Are there supermarkets in Sydney and is milk available all year round? (Germany)
A: No, we are a peaceful civilization of vegan hunter/gatherers. Milk is illegal.

Q: Please send a list of all doctors in Australia who can dispense rattlesnake serum. (USA)
A: Rattlesnakes live in A-mer-ica, which is where YOU come from. All Australian snakes are perfectly harmless, can be safely handled, and make good pets.

Q: I have a question about a famous animal in Australia, but I forget its name. It's a kind of bear and lives in trees. (USA)

A: It's called a Drop Bear. They are so called because they drop out of gum trees and eat the brains of anyone walking underneath them. You can scare them off by spraying yourself with human urine before you go out walking.

Q: I have developed a new product that is the fountain of youth. Can you tell me where I can sell it in Australia? (USA)
A: Anywhere significant numbers of Americans gather.

Q: Do you celebrate Christmas in Australia? (France)
A: Only at Christmas.

Q: Will I be able to speak English most places I go? (USA)
A: Yes, but you'll have to learn it first.

☺ @ ☺

Naval extracts of Officers reports:

1. His men would follow him anywhere, but only out of curiosity.

2. I would not breed from this Officer.

3. This man is depriving a village somewhere of its idiot.

4. This officer can be likened to a small puppy - he runs around excitedly, leaving little messes for other people to clean up.

5. This Officer is really not so much of a has-been, more of a definitely won't-be.

6. When she opens her mouth, it seems only to change whichever foot was previously in there.

7. Couldn't organise 50% leave in a 2 man submarine

8. He has carried out each and every one of his duties to his entire satisfaction.

9. He would be out of his depth in a car park puddle.

10. Technically sound, but socially impossible.

11. The occasional flashes of adequacy are marred by an attitude of apathy and indifference.

12. When he joined my ship, this Officer was something of a granny; since then he has aged considerably.

13. This Medical Officer has used my ship to carry his genitals from port to port, and my officers to carry him from bar to bar.

14. This Officer reminds me very much of a gyroscope, always spinning around at a frantic pace, but not really going anywhere.

15. Since my last report he has reached rock bottom, and has started to dig.

16. She sets low personal standards and then consistently fails to achieve them.

17. He has the wisdom of youth, and the energy of old age.

18. This Officer should go far, and the sooner he starts, the better.

19. In my opinion this pilot should not be authorised to fly below 250 feet.

20. The only ship I would recommend for this man is citizenship.

21. Couldn't organise a woodpecker's picnic in Sherwood Forest.

22. Works well when under constant supervision and cornered like a rat in a trap.

23. Not the sharpest knife in the drawer.

24. Gates are down, the lights are flashing, but the train isn't coming.

25. Has two brains; one is lost and the other out looking for it.

26. If he were any more stupid, he'd have to be watered twice a week.

27. Got into the gene pool while the lifeguard wasn't watching.

28. If you stand close enough to him, you can hear the ocean.

29. It's hard to believe that he beat 1,000,000 other sperm.

30. A room temperature IQ.

31. Got a full 6-pack, but lacks the plastic thingy to hold it all together.

32. A gross ignoramus, 143 times worse than an ordinary ignoramus.

33. He has a photographic memory but has the lens cover glued on.

34. He has been working with glue too long.

35. When his IQ reaches 50, he should sell.

36. This man hasn't got enough grey matter to sole the flip-flop of a one legged budgie.

37. If two people are talking, and one looks bored, he's the other one.

38. One-celled organisms would out score him in an IQ test.

39. He donated his body to science before he finished using it.

40. Fell out of the stupid tree and hit every branch on the way down.

41. He's so dense, light bends around him.

42. If brains were taxed, he'd get a rebate.

43. Some drink from the fountain of knowledge; he only gargled.

44. Takes him 1.1/2 hours to watch 60 minutes.

45. Wheel is turning, but the hamster is long dead.

☺ @ ☺

This is a story of self control and marksmanship by a brave, cool-headed woman with a small pistol against a fierce predator. What is the smallest calibre that you would trust to protect yourself?

A Beretta Jetfire testimonial

Here is her story:
While out walking along the edge of a bayou just below Houma, Louisiana with my soon to be ex-husband discussing property settlement and other divorce issues, we were surprised by a huge 12-ft. Alligator that suddenly emerged from the murky water and charging us with its large jaws wide open. She must have been protecting her nest because she was extremely aggressive.

If I had not had my little Beretta Jetfire .25 calibre pistol with me I would not be here today!

Just one shot to my estranged husband's knee cap was all it took. The 'gator got him easily and I was able to escape by just walking away at a brisk pace. It's one of the best pistols in my collection! Plus ... The amount I saved in lawyer's fees was more than worth the purchase price of the gun.

☺ @ ☺

THAT'S THE SPIRIT . . .

[Billboard image: "This year thousands of men will die from stubbornness." with graffiti added: "NO WE WON'T"]

☺ @ ☺

For those who love the philosophy of ambiguity

1. If man evolved from monkeys and apes, why do we still have monkeys and apes?

2. I went to a bookstore and asked the saleswoman, "Where's the self-help section?" She said if she told me, it would defeat the purpose.

3. What if there were no hypothetical questions?

4. If someone with multiple personalities threatens to kill himself, is it considered a hostage situation?

5. Is there another word for synonym?

6. Where do forest rangers go to "get away from it all?"

7. What do you do when you see an endangered animal eating an endangered plant?

8. Would a fly without wings be called a walk?

9. Why do they lock petrol station toilets? Are they afraid someone will clean them?

10. If a turtle doesn't have a shell, is he homeless or naked?

12. What was the best thing before sliced bread?

13. One nice thing about egotists: they don't talk about other people.

14. How is it possible to have a civil war?

15. If one synchronized swimmer drowns, do the rest drown too?

16. If you try to fail, and succeed, which have you done?

17. Whose cruel idea was it for the word "Lisp" to have "S" in it?

18. Why is it called tourist season if we can't shoot at them?

19. Why is there an expiration date on sour cream?

20. If you spin an oriental man in a circle three times does he become disoriented?

☺ @ ☺

British Humour

The train was quite crowded, a U.S. Marine walked the entire length looking for a seat, but the only seat left was taken by a poodle belonging to a well dressed, middle-aged, French woman.
The war-weary Marine asked, "Ma'am, may I have that seat?"
The French woman just sniffed and said to no one in particular, "Americans are so rude. My little Fifi is using that seat."
The Marine walked the entire train again, but the only seat left was under that dog. "Please, ma'am. May I sit down? I'm very tired."
She snorted, "Not only are you Americans rude, you are also arrogant!"
This time the Marine didn't say a word. He just picked up the little dog, tossed it out the train window, and sat down.
The woman shrieked, "I'm horrified. Someone must defend my honour and put this American in his place!"
An English gentleman sitting nearby spoke up, "Sir, you Americans seem to have a penchant for doing the wrong thing. You hold the fork in the wrong hand. You drive your cars on the wrong side of the road. And now, sir, you seem to have thrown the wrong bitch out the window."

☺ @ ☺

THE PERFECT HUSBAND

Several men are in the locker room of a golf club.
A cell phone on a bench rings and a man engages the hands free speaker function and begins to talk.
Everyone else in the room stops to listen.

MAN: 'Hello'
WOMAN: 'Honey, it's me. Are you at the club?'
MAN: 'Yes'
WOMAN: 'I am at the mall now and found this beautiful leather coat. It's only $1,000. Is it OK if I buy it?'
MAN: 'Sure, go ahead if you like it that much.'
WOMAN: 'I also stopped by the Mercedes dealership and saw the new 2008 models. I saw one I really liked.'
MAN: 'How much?'
WOMAN: '$390,000'
MAN: 'OK, but for that price I want it with all the options.'
WOMAN: 'Great! Oh, and one more thing...the house I wanted last year is back on the market. They're asking $2,950,000' for it.
MAN: 'Well, then go ahead and give them an offer of $2,800,000. They will probably take it. If not, we can go the extra $150,000 if it's really a pretty good price.'
WOMAN: 'OK. I'll see you later! I love you so much!'
MAN: 'Bye! I love you, too.'
The man hangs up. The other men in the locker room are staring at him in astonishment, mouths agape.
He turns and asks: 'Anyone know who this phone belongs to?'

☺ @ ☺

When the white missionaries came to Africa they had the Bible and we had the land. They said 'Let us pray.' We closed our eyes. When we opened them we had the Bible and they had the land.

~ Desmond Tutu

☺ @ ☺

WHY MEN HAVE BETTER FRIENDS...

Friendship Between Women:

A woman didn't come home one night. The next day she told her husband that she had slept over at a friend's house. The man called his wife's 10 best friends. None of them knew about it.

Friendship between Men:

A man didn't come home one night. The next day he told his wife that he had slept over at a friend's house. The woman called her husband's 10 best friends. Eight of them confirmed that he had slept over, and two claimed that he was still there.

☺ @ ☺

Remember: You don't stop laughing because you grow old, You grow old because you stop laughing.

☺ @ ☺

CAN YOU GET MARRIED IN HEAVEN?

On their way to get married, a young Catholic couple is involved in a fatal car accident. They find themselves sitting outside the Pearly Gates, waiting for St. Peter to process them into Heaven.
While waiting, they begin to wonder: Could they possibly get married in Heaven? When St. Peter shows up, they ask him.
St. Peter says, 'I don't know. This is the first time anyone has asked that. Let me go and find out,' and he leaves.
The couple sit and wait, and wait. Two months pass and the couple is still waiting. As they wait, they discuss that if they were allowed to get married in Heaven, what was the eternal aspect of it all. 'What if it doesn't work?' they wondered. 'Are we stuck together forever?'

After yet another month, St. Peter finally returns, looking somewhat bedraggled. 'Yes,' he informs the couple, 'you can get married in Heaven.'

'Great!' says the couple, 'But we were just wondering, what if things don't work out? Can we also get a divorce in Heaven?'

St. Peter, red-faced with anger, slams his clipboard onto the ground.

'What's wrong?' ask the frightened couple.

'OH, COME ON!' St. Peter shouts, 'It took me three months to find a priest up here! Do you have any idea how long it'll take me to find a lawyer?'

☺ @ ☺

OLD DOG

A wealthy Old Gentleman decides to go on a hunting safari in Africa, taking his faithful, elderly dog named Killer, along for the company.

One day the old dog starts chasing rabbits and before long, discovers that he's lost. Wandering about, he notices a leopard heading rapidly in his direction with the intention of having lunch.

The old dog thinks, "Oh, oh! I'm in deep doo-doo now!" Noticing some bones on the ground close by, he immediately settles down to chew on the bones with his back to the approaching cat. Just as the leopard is about to leap, the old dog exclaims loudly, "Boy, that was one delicious leopard! I wonder, if there are any more around here?"

Hearing this, the young leopard halts his attack in mid-strike, a look of terror comes over him and he slinks away into the trees. "Whew", says the leopard, "That was close"! That old dog nearly had me!"

Meanwhile, a monkey who had been watching the whole scene from a nearby tree, figures he can put this knowledge to good use and trade it for protection from the leopard. So, off he goes, but the old dog sees him heading after the leopard with great speed, and figures that something must be up.

The monkey soon catches up with the leopard, spills the beans and strikes a deal for himself with the leopard.

The young leopard is furious at being made a fool of and says, "Here, monkey, hop on my back and see what's going to happen to that conniving canine!"

Now, the old dog sees the leopard coming with the monkey on his back and thinks, "What am I going to do now?" But instead of running, the dog sits down with his back to his attackers, pretending he hasn't seen them yet, and just when they get close enough to hear, the old dog says...
"Where's that damn monkey? I sent him off an hour ago to bring me another leopard"!

Moral of this story...
Don't mess with the old dogs... age and skill will always overcome youth and treachery! Brilliance only comes with age and experience.

☺ @ ☺

COINCIDENCE

Two guys are trying to get in a quick eighteen holes, but there are two terrible lady golfers in front of them hitting the ball everywhere but where it's supposed to go.
The first guy says, "Why don't you go over and ask if we can play through?" The second guy gets about halfway there, turns and comes back.
The first guy says, "What's wrong?"
He says, "One of them is my wife, and the other one is my mistress."
The first guy says, "That could be a problem. I'll go over."
He gets about halfway there and he turns and comes back, too.
The second guy says, "What's wrong?"
The first guy says, "Small world."

☺ @ ☺

HUSBAND DAY CARE CENTER
- NEED TIME TO RELAX?
- NEED TIME TO YOURSELF?
- WANT TO GO SHOPPING?

LEAVE YOUR HUSBAND WITH US!
WE LOOK AFTER HIM FOR YOU!
YOU ONLY PAY FOR HIS DRINKS!

☺ @ ☺

GRANDMOTHERS DON'T KNOW EVERYTHING

Tony was 9 years old and was staying with his grandmother for a few days.
He'd been playing outside with the other kids, when he came into the house and asked her, 'Grandma, what's that called when two people sleep in the same bedroom and one is on top of the other?' She was a little taken aback, but she decided to tell him the truth. 'Well, dear, it's called sexual intercourse.' 'Oh,' Little Tony said, 'OK,' and went back outside to play with the other kids.
A few minutes later he came back in and said angrily, 'Grandma, it isn't called sexual intercourse. It's called Bunk Beds. And Jimmy's mum wants to talk to you.'

☺ @ ☺

What have we learned in 2,064 years?

"The budget should be balanced, the Treasury should be refilled, public debt should be reduced, the arrogance of officialdom should be tempered and controlled, and the assistance to foreign lands should be curtailed lest Rome become bankrupt. People must again learn to work, instead of living on public assistance."

- Cicero - 55 BC

Evidently nothing...!

☺   @   ☺

Best of Africa's 2009 true News Stories!

1. The Cape Times (Cape Town)

"I have promised to keep his identity confidential,' said Jack Maxim, a spokeswoman for the Sandton Sun Hotel, Johannesburg , "but I can confirm that he is no longer in our employment. We asked him to clean the lifts and he spent four days on the job. When I asked him why, he replied: 'Well, there are forty of them, two on each floor and sometimes some of them aren't there'. Eventually, we realised that he thought each floor had a different lift, and he'd cleaned the same two twelve times. "We had to let him go. It seemed best all round. I understand he is now working for Escom."

2. The Star (Johannesburg)

"The situation is absolutely under control," Transport Minister Ephraem Magagula told the Swaziland Parliament in Mbabane . "Our nation's merchant navy is perfectly safe. We just don't know where it is, that's all." Replying to an MP's question, Minister Magagula admitted that the landlocked country had completely lost track of its only ship, the Swazimar.

"We believe it is in a sea somewhere. At one time, we sent a team of men to look for it, but there was a problem with drink and they failed to find it, and so, technically, yes, we've lost it a bit. But I categorically reject all suggestions of incompetence on the part of this government. The Swazimar is a big ship painted in the sort of nice bright colours you can see at night. Mark my words, it will turn up. The right honourable gentleman opposite is a very naughty man, and he will laugh on the other side of his face when my ship comes in."

3. The Standard (Kenya)

"What is all the fuss about?" Weseka Sambu asked a hastily convened news conference at Jomo Kenyatta International Airport . "A technical hitch like this could have happened anywhere in the world. You people are not patriots You just want to cause trouble." Sambu, a spokesman for Kenya Airways, was speaking after the cancellation of a through flight from Kisumu, via Jomo Kenyatta, to Berlin .

"The forty-two passengers had boarded the plane ready for take-off, when the pilot noticed one of the tyres was flat. Kenya Airways did not possess a spare tyre, and unfortunately the airport nitrogen canister was empty. A passenger suggested taking the tyre to a petrol station for inflation, but unluckily the jack had gone missing so we couldn't get the wheel off. Our engineers tried heroically to re-inflate the tyre with a bicycle pump, but had no luck, and the pilot even blew into the valve with his mouth, but he passed out. "When I announced that the flight had to be abandoned, one of the passengers, Mr Mutu, suddenly struck me about the face with a life-jacket whistle and said we were a national disgrace. I told him he was being ridiculous, and that there was to be another flight in a fortnight.

And, in the meantime, he would be able to enjoy the scenery around Kisumu, albeit at his own expense."

4. From a Zimbabwean newspaper

While transporting mental patients from Harare to Bulawayo, the bus Driver stopped at a roadside shebeen (beerhall) for a few beers.

When he got back to his vehicle, he found it empty, with the 20 patients nowhere to be seen. Realizing the trouble he was in if the truth were uncovered, he halted his bus at the next bus stop and offered lifts to those in the queue. Letting 20 people board, he then shut the doors and drove straight to the Bulawayo mental hospital, where he hastily handed over his 'charges', warning the nurses that they were particularly excitable. Staff removed the furious passengers; it was three days later that suspicions were roused by the consistency of stories from the 20. As for the real patients: nothing more has been heard of them and they have apparently blended comfortably back into Zimbabwean society.

☺ @ ☺

NO WORDS NEEDED

☺ @ ☺

THINGS ARE NOT ALWAYS AS THEY SEEM . .

A man met a beautiful blonde lady and decided he wanted to marry her right away.

She said, 'But we don't know anything about each other.'

He said, 'That's all right, we'll learn about each other as we go along.'

So she consented, they were married, and off they went on a honeymoon at a very nice resort.

One morning they were lying by the pool, when he got up off of his towel, climbed up to the 10 metre board and did a two and a half tuck, followed by three rotations in the pike position, at which point he straightened out and cut the water like a knife.

After a few more demonstrations, he came back and lay down on the towel.

She said, 'That was incredible!'

He said, 'I used to be an Olympic diving champion. You see, I told you we'd learn more about each other as we went along.'

So she got up, jumped in the pool and started doing lengths.

After seventy-five lengths she climbed out of the pool, lay down on her towel and was hardly out of breath.

He said, 'That was incredible! Were you an Olympic endurance swimmer?'

'No,' she said, 'I was a prostitute in Liverpool but I worked both sides of the Mersey

☺ @ ☺

BRITISH NEWSPAPERS

Commenting on a complaint from a Mr. Arthur Purdey about a large gas bill, a spokesman for North West Gas said, 'We agree it was rather high for the time of year. It's possible Mr. Purdey has been charged for the gas used up during the explosion that destroyed his house.'
(The Daily Telegraph)

Irish police are being handicapped in a search for a stolen van, because they cannot issue a description. It's a Special Branch vehicle and they don't want the public to know what it looks like.
(The Guardian)

A young girl who was blown out to sea on a set of inflatable teeth was rescued by a man on an inflatable lobster.
A coast guard spokesman commented, 'This sort of thing is all too common'.
(The Times)

At the height of the gale, the harbourmaster radioed a coast guard and asked him to estimate the wind speed. He replied he was sorry, but he didn't have a gauge.
However, if it was any help, the wind had just blown his Land Rover off the cliff.
(Aberdeen Evening Express)

Mrs. Irene Graham of Thorpe Avenue , Boscombe, delighted the audience with her reminiscence of the German prisoner of war who was sent each week to do her garden. He was repatriated at the end of 1945, she recalled -
'He'd always seemed a nice friendly chap, but when the crocuses came up in the middle of our lawn in February 1946, they spelt out 'Heil Hitler."
(Bournemouth Evening Echo)

☺ @ ☺

MUM'S DRIVING LICENCE

A mother is driving her little girl to her friend's house for a play day.
'Mummy ,' the little girl asks, 'how old are you?'
'Honey, you are not supposed to ask a lady her age,' the mother replied. 'It's not polite.'
'OK', the little girl says, 'What colour was your hair two years ago?
'Now really,' the mother says, 'those are personal questions and are really none of your business.'
Undaunted, the little girl asks, 'Why did you and Daddy get a divorce?'
'That's enough questions young lady! Honestly!'
The exasperated mother walks away as the two friends begin to play.
'My Mum won't tell me anything about herself,' the little girl says to her friend.
'WELL' says the friend, 'all you need to do is look at her Driving licence'.
It's like our report cards, it has everything on it.'
Later that night the little girl says to her mother, 'I know how old you are. You are 32.'
The mother is surprised and asks, 'How did you find that out?'
'I also know that you used to have brown hair.'
The mother is past surprised and shocked now.
'How in Heaven's name did you find that out?'
'And,' the little girl says triumphantly, 'I also know why you and daddy got a divorce.'
'Oh really' says the mother.......Why?

'It's all on your driving licence and you got an 'F' in sex.

☺ @ ☺

We are here on earth to do good unto others. What the others are here for, I have no idea.
~ WH Auden

☺ @ ☺

EATING IN THE FIFTIES

Pasta had not been invented.
Curry was a surname.
A takeaway was a mathematical problem.
A pizza was something to do with a leaning tower.
Bananas and oranges only appeared at Christmas time.
All crisps were plain; the only choice we had was whether to put the salt on or not.
A Chinese chippy was a foreign carpenter.
Rice was a milk pudding, and never, ever part of our dinner.
A Big Mac was what we wore when it was raining.
Brown bread was something only poor people ate.
Oil was for lubricating, fat was for cooking
Tea was made in a teapot using tea leaves and never green.
Coffee only came with chicory, and came in a bottle.
Cubed sugar was regarded as posh.
Only Heinz made beans.
Fish didn't have fingers in those days.
Eating raw fish was called poverty, not sushi.
None of us had ever heard of yogurt.
Healthy food consisted of anything edible.
People who didn't peel potatoes were regarded as lazy.
Indian restaurants were only found in India .
Cooking outside was called camping.
Seaweed was not a recognised food.
"Kebab" was not even a word never mind a food.
Sugar enjoyed a good press in those days, and was regarded as being white gold.
Prunes were medicinal.
Surprisingly muesli was available, it was called cattle feed.
Water came out of the tap, if someone had suggested bottling it and charging more than petrol for it they would have become a laughing stock.
The one thing that we never ever had on our table in the fifties .. was elbows!

☺ @ ☺

TIME

Time is like a river. You cannot touch the water twice, because the flow that has passed will never pass again. Enjoy every moment of life. As a bagpiper, I play many gigs. Recently I was asked by a funeral director to play at a graveside service for a homeless man.

He had no family or friends, so the service was to be at a pauper's cemetery in the Nova Scotia back country.

As I was not familiar with the backwoods, I got lost and, being a typical man, I didn't stop for directions.

I finally arrived an hour late and saw the funeral guy had evidently gone and the hearse was nowhere in sight. There were only the diggers and crew left and they were eating lunch. I felt badly and apologized to the men for being late.

I went to the side of the grave and looked down and the vault lid was already in place. I didn't know what else to do, so I started to play.

The workers put down their lunches and began to gather around. I played out my heart and soul for this man with no family and friends. I played like I've never played before for this homeless man.

And as I played "Amazing Grace", the workers began to weep. They wept, I wept, we all wept together. When I finished, I packed up my bagpipes and started for my car. Though my head was hung low, my heart was full.

As I opened the door to my car, I heard one of the workers say, "I never seen nothing like that before and I've been putting in septic tanks for twenty years."

☺ @ ☺

POLITICIANS

We hang petty thieves and appoint the great ones to public office.
>~Aesop, Greek slave & fable author

Those who are too smart to engage in politics are punished by being governed by those who are dumber.
>~Plato, ancient Greek Philosopher

Politicians are the same all over. They promise to build a bridge even where there is no river.
>~Nikita Khrushchev, Russian Soviet politician

Politicians are people who, when they see light at the end of the tunnel, go out and buy some more tunnel.
>~John Quinton, American actor/writer

Politics is the gentle art of getting votes from the poor and campaign funds from the rich, by promising to protect each from the other.
>~Oscar Ameringer, "the Mark Twain of American Socialism."

I offered my opponents a deal: "if they stop telling lies about me, I will stop telling the truth about them".
>~Adlai Stevenson, campaign speech, 1952.

A politician is a fellow who will lay down your life for his country.
>~Texas Guinan. 19th century American businessman

I have come to the conclusion that politics is too serious a matter to be Left to the politicians.
>~Charles de Gaulle, French general & politician

Instead of giving a politician the keys to the city, it might be better to change the locks.
>~Doug Larson

IF YOU WERE AROUND IN 1919 AND SAW THIS POSTER

LIPS THAT TOUCH LIQUOR SHALL NOT TOUCH OURS

WOULDN'T YOU JUST KEEP ON DRINKING?

☺ @ ☺

SHE MAY BE RIGHT...

A Sunday school teacher asked her little children, as they were on the way to church service, "And why is it necessary to be quiet in church?" One bright little girl replied, "Because people are sleeping."

☺ @ ☺

MAGIC

A Yorkshireman and a Scouser go into Greggs the bakers.

The Scouser nicks 3 pies and puts them in his pocket, then boasts to the Yorkshire guy, "Did you see that? The staff never even saw me."

The Yorkshireman says, "That's nowt mate, watch this."

So the Yorkshireman goes back into the shop and says to the manager, "Gi'us a pie and I'll show thee some magic," and eats the pie in front of him, and then does it twice more.

The manager says, "So, where's the magic in that?"

The Yorkshire guy says, "Go and check that Scouser's pocket."

☺ @ ☺

OUT OF THE MOUTHS OF BABES . . .

An Elementary School Teacher had twenty six children in her first grade class (six year olds). She presented each child with the first half of a well-known proverb and asked them to come up with the remainder of the proverb.

It's hard to believe these were actually done by first graders. Their insight may surprise you.

While reading, bear in mind that these are only six year olds, because the last one is a classic!

1. Don't change horses. . . . . until they stop running.
2. Strike while . . . . the bug is close.
3. It's always darkest before. . . . . Daylight Saving Time.
4. Never underestimate the power of . . . . termites.

5. You can lead a horse to water but . . . . how?
6. Don't bite the hand that . . . . looks dirty.
7. No news is . . . . impossible.
8. A miss is as good as a . . . . Mr.
9. You can't teach an old dog . . . . .new math.
10. If you lie down with dogs, ...you'll stink in the morning.
11. Love all, trust . . . . me.
12. The pen is mightier than the . . . . .pigs.
13. An idle mind is . . . . the best way to relax.
14. Where there's smoke there's . . . . pollution.
15. Happy the bride who . . . . gets all the presents.
16. A penny saved is . . . . not much.
17. Two's company, three's . . . . .the Musketeers.
18. Don't put off till tomorrow what . . you put on to go to bed
19. Laugh and the whole world laughs with you, cry and
. . . . you have to blow your nose.
20. There are none so blind as . . . . Stevie Wonder.
21. Children should be seen and not . . . spanked or grounded.
22. If at first you don't succeed . . . . get new batteries.
23. You get out of something only what you
. . . . see in the picture on the box.
24. When the blind lead the blind . . . . get out of the way.
25. A bird in the hand . . . . is going to poop on you.

And the WINNER and last one!

26. Better late than . . . . pregnant.

☺ @ ☺

FROZEN WINDOWS

Wife by text to husband at work . . . .
"Windows at home frozen - what should I do?"
Husband - "spray some de-icer or pour hot water on them"
Wife a few minutes later - "Done that - now computer won't work at all"!

☺ @ ☺

OUT OF MORE MOUTHS...

HISTORY

In wartime children who lived in big cities had to be evaporated because it was safer in the country.

MATHS

The total is when you add up all the numbers and a remainder is an animal that pulls santa on his slay.

THE ARTS

In last year's ~~xmas~~ Christmas concert, Linzi played the main prat. I played one of the smaller prats and I would like to have a bigger prat this year.

MATHS

If it is less than 90 degrees it is a cute angel.

SCIENCE

Helicopters are cleverer than planes. Not only can they fly through the air they can also hoover.

HOLIDAYS

On our activity holiday Dad wanted to ride the hores, but mom said they were too ekspensiv.

THE ARTS

... and at the end of the show we all sing away in a manager.

GEOGRAPHY

In Scandinavia, the Danish people come from Denmark, the Norwegians come from Norway and the Lapdancers come from Lapland.

HISTORY

SOMETIMES IN THE WAR THEY TAKE PRISNERS AND KEEP THEM AS OSTRIGES UNTIL THE WAR IS OVER. SOME PRISNERS END UP IN CONSTERPATION CAMPS.

RELIGIOUS STUDIES

A mosque is a sort of church. The main difference is that its roof is doomed.

NO PARENT LEFT BEHIND.....

These are real notes written by parents in the Memphis school district .

Spellings have been left intact......

1. My son is under a doctor's care and should not take PE today. Please execute him.

2. Please exkuce lisa for being absent she was sick and i had her shot.

3. Dear school: please ecsc's john being absent on jan. 28, 29, 30, 31, 32 and also 33.

4. Please excuse gloria from jim today. She is administrating.

5. Please excuse roland from p.e. for a few days. Yesterday he fell out of a tree and misplaced his hip.

6. John has been absent because he had two teeth taken out of his face.

7. Carlos was absent yesterday because he was playing football. He was hurt in the growing part.

8. Megan could not come to school today because she has been bothered by very close veins.

9. Chris will not be in school cus he has an acre in his side.

10. Please excuse ray Friday from school. He has very loose vowels.

11. Please excuse Lesli from being absent yesterday. She had ~~diahre dyrea direathe~~ the shits.

12. Please excuse tommy for being absent yesterday.. He had diarrhea, and his boots leak.

13. Irving was absent yesterday because he missed his bust.

14. Please excuse jimmy for being. It was his father's fault.

15. I kept Billie home because she had to go Christmas shopping because i don't know what size she wear.

16. Please excuse jennifer for missing school yesterday. We forgot to get the sunday paper off the porch, and when we found it monday. We thought it was sunday.

17. Sally won't be in school a week from friday. We have to attend her funeral.

18. My daughter was absent yesterday because she was tired. She spent a weekend with the marines.

19. Please excuse Jason for being absent yesterday. He had a cold and could not breed well.

20. Please excuse mary for being absent yesterday. She was in bed with gramps.

21. Gloria was absent yesterday as she was having a gangover.

22. Please excuse brenda. She has been sick and under the doctor.

23. Maryann was absent december 11-16, because she had a fever, sorethroat, headache and upset stomach. Her sister was also sick, fever an sore throat, her brother had a low grade fever and ached all over. I wasn't the best either, sore throat and fever. There must be something going around, her father even got hot last night.

☺ @ ☺

DID I READ THAT SIGN RIGHT?

TOILET OUT OF ORDER. PLEASE USE FLOOR BELOW

In a Laundromat:
AUTOMATIC WASHING MACHINES: PLEASE REMOVE ALL YOUR CLOTHES WHEN THE LIGHT GOES OUT

In a London department store:
BARGAIN BASEMENT UPSTAIRS

In an office:
WOULD THE PERSON WHO TOOK THE STEP LADDER YESTERDAY PLEASE BRING IT BACK OR FURTHER STEPS WILL BE TAKEN

In an office:
AFTER TEA BREAK STAFF SHOULD EMPTY THE TEAPOT AND STAND UPSIDE DOWN ON THE DRAINING BOARD

Outside a second-hand shop:
WE EXCHANGE ANYTHING - BICYCLES, WASHING MACHINES, ETC. WHY NOT BRING YOUR WIFE ALONG AND GET A WONDERFUL BARGAIN?

Notice in health food shop window:
CLOSED DUE TO ILLNESS

Spotted in a safari park:
ELEPHANTS PLEASE STAY IN YOUR CAR

Seen during a conference:
FOR ANYONE WHO HAS CHILDREN AND DOESN'T KNOW IT, THERE IS A DAY CARE ON THE FIRST FLOOR

Notice in a farmer's field:
THE FARMER ALLOWS WALKERS TO CROSS THE FIELD FOR FREE, BUT THE BULL CHARGES.

Message on a leaflet:
IF YOU CANNOT READ, THIS LEAFLET WILL TELL YOU HOW TO GET LESSONS

On a repair shop door:
WE CAN REPAIR ANYTHING. (PLEASE KNOCK HARD ON THE DOOR - THE BELL DOESN'T WORK)

☺ @ ☺

Police Warning

Watch Out For This Scam

Police say that the gang is usually comprised of four members, one adult and three younger ones.
While the three younger ones, all appearing sweet and innocent, divert their 'mark' (or intended target) with a show of friendliness , the fourth - the eldest -- sneaks in from behind the person's back to expertly rifle through his or her pockets and purses or bags for any valuables being carried.

The picture below shows the gang in operation.

☺ @ ☺

ACTUAL CALL CENTRE CONVERSATIONS

Customer: 'I've been ringing 0800 2100 for two days and can't get through to enquiries, can you help?'.
Operator: 'Where did you get that number from, sir?'.
Customer: 'It was on the door to the Travel Centre'.
Operator: 'Sir, they are our opening hours'.

Samsung Electronics
Caller: 'Can you give me the telephone number for Jack?'
Operator: 'I'm sorry, sir, I don't understand who you are talking about'.
Caller: 'On page 1, section 5, of the user guide it clearly states that I need to unplug the fax machine from the AC wall socket and telephone Jack before cleaning. Now, can you give me the number for Jack?'
Operator: 'I think you mean the telephone point on the wall'.

RAC Motoring Services
Caller: 'Does your European Breakdown Policy cover me when I am travelling in Australia?'
Operator: ' Doesn't the product name give you a clue?'

Caller (enquiring about legal requirements while travelling in France):
'If I register my car in France, do I have to change the steering wheel to the other side of the car?'

Directory Enquiries
Caller: 'I'd like the number of the Argoed Fish Bar in Cardiff please'.
Operator: 'I'm sorry, there's no listing. Is the spelling correct?'
Caller: 'Well, it used to be called the Bargoed Fish Bar but the 'B' fell off'.

Then there was the caller who asked for a knitwear company in Woven.
Operator: 'Woven? Are you sure?'
Caller: 'Yes. That's what it says on the label; Woven in Scotland '.

On another occasion, a man making heavy breathing sounds from a phone box told a worried operator:
'I haven't got a pen, so I'm steaming up the window to write the number on'.
Tech Support: 'I need you to right-click on the Open Desktop'.
Customer: 'OK'..
Tech Support: 'Did you get a pop-up menu?'.
Customer: 'No'.
Tech Support: 'OK. Right-Click again. Do you see a pop-up menu?'
Customer: 'No'.
Tech Support: 'OK, sir. Can you tell me what you have done up until this point? '.
Customer: 'Sure. You told me to write 'click' and I wrote 'click".

Tech Support: 'OK. In the bottom left hand side of the screen, can you see the 'OK' button displayed?'
Customer: 'Wow. How can you see my screen from there?'

Caller: 'I deleted a file from my PC last week and I have just realised that I need it. If I turn my system clock back two weeks will I have my file back again? '.

☺ @ ☺

I think this next chap should have been promoted, not fired. This is next example is a true story from the Word Perfect Helpline, which was transcribed from a recording monitoring the customer care department. . . .

Needless to say the Help Desk employee was fired; however, he/she is currently suing the Word Perfect organization for 'Termination without Cause'.

Actual dialogue of a former WordPerfect Customer Support employee. (Now I know why they record these conversations!):

Operator: 'Ridge Hall, computer assistance; may I help you?'
Caller: 'Yes, well, I'm having trouble with WordPerfect.'
Operator: 'What sort of trouble?'
Caller: 'Well, I was just typing along, and all of a sudden the words went away.'
Operator: 'Went away?'
Caller: 'They disappeared.'
Operator: 'Hmm So what does your screen look like now?'
Caller: 'Nothing.'
Operator: 'Nothing?'
Caller: 'It's blank; it won't accept anything when I type.'
Operator: 'Are you still in WordPerfect, or did you get out?'
Caller: 'How do I tell?'
Operator: 'Can you see the C: prompt on the screen?'
Caller: 'What's a sea-prompt?'
Operator: 'Never mind, can you move your cursor around the screen?'
Caller: 'There isn't any cursor: I told you, it won't accept anything I type.'
Operator: 'Does your monitor have a power indicator?'
Caller: 'What's a monitor?'
Operator: 'It's the thing with the screen on it that looks like a TV. Does it have a little light that tells you when it's on?'
Caller: 'I don't know.'
Operator: 'Well, then look on the back of the monitor and find where the power cord goes into it. Can you see that?'
Caller: 'Yes, I think so.'
Operator: 'Great. Follow the cord to the plug, and tell me if it's plugged into the wall.
Caller: 'Yes, it is.'

Operator: 'When you were behind the monitor, did you notice that there were two cables plugged into the back of it, not just one?'
Caller: 'No.'
Operator: 'Well, there are. I need you to look back there again and find the other cable.'
Caller: 'Okay, here it is.'
Operator: 'Follow it for me, and tell me if it's plugged securely into the back of your computer.'
Caller: 'I can't reach.'
Operator: 'Uh huh. Well, can you see if it is?'
Caller: 'No.'
Operator: 'Even if you maybe put your knee on something and lean way over?'
Caller: 'Oh, it's not because I don't have the right angle - it's because it's dark.'
Operator: 'Dark?'
Caller: 'Yes - the office light is off, and the only light I have is coming in from the window.'
Operator: 'Well, turn on the office light then.'
Caller: 'I can't.'
Operator: 'No? Why not?'
Caller: 'Because there's a power failure.'
Operator: 'A power......... A power failure? Aha, Okay, we've got it licked now. Do you still have the boxes and manuals and packing stuff your computer came in?'
Caller: 'Well, yes, I keep them in the closet.'
Operator: 'Good. Go get them, and unplug your system and pack it up just like it was when you got it. Then take it back to the store you bought it from.'
Caller: 'Really? Is it that bad?'
Operator: 'Yes, I'm afraid it is.'
Caller: 'Well, all right then, I suppose. What do I tell them?'
Operator: 'Tell them you're too stupid to own a computer!!!!!'

☺ @ ☺

ANGELA MERKEL

SUPERGLUE
Be careful with it...

☺ @ ☺

GRAMMAR

"In English, there is no double positive that makes a negative."
"Yeah, right."

☺ @ ☺

Made in the USA
Charleston, SC
30 August 2014